THE
MESSAGE OF
ASTROLOGY

In the same series:
ASTROLOGICAL HEALING
Reinhold Ebertin
ASTROLOGY ALIVE!
Barbara Schermer
RELATIONSHIPS, ASTROLOGY AND KARMA
Pauline Stone

THE MESSAGE OF ASTROLOGY

The New Vitalism and What It Means for Our Future

PETER ROBERTS

THE AQUARIAN PRESS

First published 1990

British Library Cataloguing in Publication Data

Roberts, Peter
The message of astrology. — (Aquarian new directions
in astrology)
I. Title
133.5

ISBN 0-85030-823-2

*The Aquarian Press is part of the Thorsons Publishing Group,
Wellingborough, Northamptonshire, NN8 2RQ, England*

Typeset by Harper Phototypesetters Limited, Northampton
Printed in Great Britain by Mackays of Chatham, Kent

1 3 5 7 9 10 8 6 4 2

DEDICATION

To the Memory of My Dear Friend John Addey

CONTENTS

FOREWORD

The other day, throwing out some letters my parents had kept, I came across one written to them when I was in my early twenties, dismissing astrology as rubbish. This view remained unchanged even when in the 1960s I became interested in psychical research; parapsychologists looked on astrology with disfavour. From time to time my disbelief would be a little shaken: once by a BBC television programme which had tested an astrologer 'blind', and found that three out of four horoscope personalities had proved to be remarkably close to the actuality; occasionally by finding that otherwise eminently sensible people took the subject seriously — in one case, to the point of checking every applicant for a job astrologically. But I did not begin to sit up and take notice until, in 1975, I read that nearly two hundred eminent scientists, including no less than eighteen Nobel prize-winners, had put their names to a manifesto denouncing astrology.

It is a fairly safe rule of thumb that when orthodox scientists join a campaign of this kind, it is because they feel threatened; and if they feel threatened, it is usually because some evidence has been emerging which upsets orthodox assumptions. So it turned out to be in this case; research conducted by Michel Gauquelin and his wife in Europe, along impeccably scientific lines, appeared to have established that there is some basis for the link between the time of birth and the state of the heavens — where the planets are, in relation to the newly born.

There followed one of the more discreditable episodes in the history of science. Charitably, Peter Roberts does not relate it; but I shall, as it helps to explain why it has been so difficult to get the facts across to the public. The American Committee for the Scientific Investigation of Claims of the Paranormal, 'CSICOP', set up what purported to be a scientific inquiry, but was in reality a hatchet job — CSICOP being a gathering of sceptics.

So scrupulously objective had the Gauquelins' work been — as Peter Roberts shows — that it was possible to repeat it in the United States in exactly the same form; and in 1977 the *Humanist* reported that the results revealed that there was no further need to take the Gauquelins seriously. Only gradually did it begin to emerge that in fact, the American results confirmed the Gauquelins', as six years later Kurtz and his fellow workers in CSICOP had to confess. Among those who had participated in the deception were distinguished American scientists such as George Abell, Professor of Astronomy at the University of California; the well-known science writer Martin Gardner; the magician Randi; and others. Yet in their embarrassment at finding their preconceptions upset, they had permitted what in effect was a smear on the Gauquelins, by pretending their work had been discredited.

They were not the only scientists to react in this way. Investigators in Belgium were caught out in a similar project and when it, too, confirmed the Gauquelins' findings, behaved in the same disgraceful fashion. The first lesson from the affair has been that orthodox scientists can become so faithful to the creed which they have embraced that they look upon it as a faith, to be protected at all costs, even to the point of behaving unscientifically; the second, that the Gauquelins' methods and their findings have survived close and hostile scientific scrutiny. As Peter Roberts is careful to stress, their work does not lend support to a great deal which passes for astrology; but it does confirm that there are influences which are sufficiently pervasive and consistent to justify the development of the beliefs, all those millennia ago, even if some of the accretions to them lack confirmation.

But *The Message of Astrology* does much more than set out the findings of the Gauquelins and others. It manages to present them in a form which allows them to be fitted in to science, as science is now itself developing, moving away from materialism towards a new form of vitalism.

The Message of Astrology, in other words, performs a dual function. It provides an introduction to astrology, with particular emphasis on recent findings and how they qualify old beliefs; and it sets the evidence in its scientific context, relating it to the theories of, for example, the biologist Rupert Sheldrake and the physicist David Bohm. Some of it will not be easy reading for anybody who, like myself, becomes glassy-eyed when required to absorb technicalities; but I have no doubt that Peter Roberts was justified in confronting us with them, and in general his commentary is admirably readable.

Diffidently, I would like to make one small point on behalf of those who, like me, read newspaper and magazine horoscopes if they happen to catch our eye. Agreed, this is not astrology; in so far as it pretends to be, it could be brought up on a charge of misrepresentation. But just occasionally, I find it works on the same principle that some Christians accept: when uncertain what course to follow, they open their Bibles at random and stick a forefinger on a paragraph, to see if the words bring guidance. It's not whether the guidance is correct that matters, but whether it rings a bell!

Brian Inglis
February 1989

1
TRADITIONAL ASTROLOGY

The Citadel of Science

This is a period when the citadel of science feels itself threatened by the forces of unreason. Of the scientific disciplines, biology is suffering the most acutely. The creationists, particularly in the United States, are enjoying a resurgence, even to the extent that biology textbooks in some states play down the role of evolution to the point that the word 'evolution' becomes hard to find. Every weakness in the orthodox system is seized upon. Those yawning gaps in the fossil record are regarded as fatal flaws and the evolution of structures (such as wings) which represent handicaps during the long period of their development is argued to be impossible through a natural selection process — which necessarily capitalizes only on advantages.

The citadel is threatened not only by attackers from without but also by traitors within its walls. The fundamentalists from the Bible Belt in the Southern United States who decry evolution are external foes. They can be 'defeated' again and again in the skirmishes of the campaign because they have no scientific power — they are outside the scientific circle. However, this cannot be said of Rupert Sheldrake who comes of an entirely respectable scientific lineage. In *A New Science of Life*[1] Sheldrake proposed the existence of morphogenetic fields which facilitate the learning process for all kinds of living creature. His book achieved early notoriety when the editor of the top scientific journal *Nature* pronounced it an ideal candidate for burning. Whereas it is ordinarily possible to dismiss such 'semi-mystical gobbledegook' without much ado, Sheldrake had the effrontery to propose means of testing his theory experimentally — thereby requiring his critics to pay some attention to the tests, rather than simply ignoring him.

No listing of examples could be entirely convincing of the truth of the statement that the citadel of science feels threatened, but a recent development adds weight to the case. There was founded in 1976 the Committee for the Scientific Investigation of Claims of the Paranormal (CSICOP). The aims of the committee appear at first sight to be laudable, but the record indicates that its purpose is to discredit (by any means) all claims, if they show any sign of being authentic.

Other Worlds

The question naturally arises of why the scientific establishment should feel threatened, of why it should deem it necessary to form an organization like CSICOP to discredit any workers in the field of the paranormal who might gain credence. The scientific enterprise has been hugely successful. In about three centuries the major disciplines of astronomy, geology, physics, chemistry and biology have brought system and order to a great variety of phenomena, deducing laws of wide general applicability so that understanding of the mechanics of the natural world has been increased profoundly. For those unable to appreciate the sheer elegance of scientific laws, there have been numerous visible and tangible products of the scientific enterprise. The genie of electricity serves our every domestic need, television is available to entertain us and jet aircraft are ready to speed us on foreign travels. With such an array of success and based on such a beautiful, coherent thought structure, it seems extraordinary that there should be any need to fend off a handful of 'cranks' who are suggesting that there is more to life than the rude mechanics of existence.

The answer is that some 'otherwordly' ideas, whose source lies back in a pre-scientific era, are remarkably persistent. Our materialist society, which educates us to respect reason and the empirical approach, which marginalizes religion and which fills our eyes and our ears with the clamour of the physical world here and now, cannot drive out entirely the whispers from another plane. To these whispers, scientific orthodoxy replies: 'Superstitions — waste no time on them.' But this raises a serious problem because someone has to decide which beliefs are to be labelled 'superstitions'. There was a time when the idea of rocks falling out of the sky was certified by learned men to be only a superstition of ignorant peasants. Later on, after some huffing and puffing, meteorites became respectable. The problem of deciding what is mere superstition does not trouble the scientific establishment, except during a brief transition, such as the period during which some scientists had come to believe in meteorites ahead of the field. At other times, those items to be regarded as superstition are categorized quite clearly and unambiguously. This has a striking parallel with the treatment of heresy by the Catholic Church. At any one time, those items which are heresies are clearly listed and no one need be in any doubt. In both establishments it is the senior members of the hierarchy who decide what goes on the list. In both establishments, persistent heretics are censured and have their privileges withdrawn.

A False Conflict

The conflict between science and the paranormal is apparent rather than real. It arises not from any incompatibility between paranormal phenomena and scientific method but because the scientific establishment behaves in many respects like a church defending the true faith, threatening those who dabble in heresies with excommunication. Because of this regrettable feature of the establishment, many investigators who have been trained in orthodox science but who nevertheless take an interest in the paranormal are deterred from pursuing that interest, resulting in much slower progress in this field than would otherwise occur.

It is not necessary to defend the faith. Nothing terrible will happen if scientists investigate unusual phenomena. Truth will out, and beliefs without substance will be discarded when the evidence accumulates. Far from defending anything and withdrawing behind the battlements, science should welcome the prospect of new fields for exploration. Even a cursory glance at physics over the last century shows how unwise it is to lay down rules for what is allowed and what is not. In the context of classical physics, the quantum theory is an amazing and nearly incredible construct. Nothing in the everyday world prepares us for the idea that energy comes in tiny discrete packets, so that a beam of light is a stream of photons. Yet the light also behaves as waves — it can be reflected, refracted and diffracted. All the experimental evidence shows that light is both a particle and a wave: depending on the circumstances and the means of detection. With the White Queen, any twentieth-century physicist can say '. . . sometimes I've believed as many as six impossible things before breakfast.'

Astrology

But astrology — the notion that the stars influence our earthly lives — that is too much for the majority of even our mentally agile physicists. Indeed there is a certain absurdity about the idea that causes it to be rejected by intellectuals generally. Yet popular interest in it remains at a high level. In the UK, of all the newspapers bought, the majority carry daily columns on 'you and your stars'. Many popular magazines have larger sections devoted to 'Sun sign' astrology, and this is separate from the specialist journals dealing with occult matters. Television audience ratings are improved by the appearance of a resident astrologer and from press advertisements it would seem that there are hundreds of consultant astrologers prepared to advise clients on the basis of indications from their horoscopes. All of which suggests a deep and persistent interest in the subject despite its being far from respectable. It does not, of course, suggest anything more profound. After all, there is also a tremendous appetite for romantic fiction and one would hardly consider that of any particular significance. However there are several reasons for taking some parts of astrology very seriously:

1. It is a study of great antiquity. Records showing elements of astrology go back at least 5,000 years.
2. Its adherents have appeared among a wide variety of peoples. The earliest records are Babylonian but we find evidence in Rome, Greece, Egypt, India, China, Japan and Mexico.
3. The main tenets of astrology have remained largely unchanged in spite of interpretation through many different cultures.

4. In recent decades a body of research findings has accumulated, particularly that of M. Gauquelin. These findings are the first really strong evidence for believing some of the astrological contentions.
5. The implications of the findings for our views of the universe and our place in it are of great importance.

It would not be true to say that Gauquelin's work has vindicated traditional astrology. He himself rejects astrology and regards his research as pointing to a new pathway in orthodox science. Indeed there are significant disparities between his findings and the traditional teachings. However, the similarities are more striking than the differences. What he has revealed is a pattern very similar to astrology but with a new and intriguing slant. If we take the sum of the modern evidence, including the Gauquelin corpus, and contemplate its integration into a complete theory, there is justification for declaring a rebirth of astrology. It is not a confirmation of traditional astrology; instead it is a coherent system of elements with a striking resemblance to its forebear, but with a firm empirical basis. One could say that the relationship between them has something in common with that between alchemy and modern chemistry.

In order to appreciate the distinction between the old and new, it is necessary to understand the main features of traditional astrology. The account which follows attempts a middle course among the separate schools. Where appropriate, the differences between individual schools are briefly sketched.

The Horoscope

There are several branches of astrological study, but the most important one is natal astrology — which deals with the birth chart or horoscope. The thesis of astrologers is that the moment of birth is highly significant, because the character of the child correlates closely with the pattern of the heavens at the moment of its birth. It is the pattern as seen from the place where the birth occurred, so that two children born at the same time but in widely separated places will have different horoscopes.

Only certain factors of the pattern are regarded as meaningful.

Of the heavenly bodies, the Sun, Moon and planets are considered but not — except in Chinese astrology — the so-called fixed stars. (There are some Western astrologers who regard certain fixed stars as having a role but this is quite a minor point.) In earlier times, the planets encompassed only Mercury, Venus, Mars, Jupiter and Saturn. Since the outer planets — Uranus, Neptune and Pluto — have been discovered, they have been incorporated into horoscopic delineation.

It is an astronomical feature of the solar system that the orbits of the planets (including the earth) all lie broadly in the same plane, called the plane of the ecliptic. Thus, as we look out from the earth, we see the planets lying along an arc across the sky. The Sun and Moon lie on this same arc and the arc lies in the plane of the ecliptic. As the planets move along the arc they appear successively in different constellations of stars and these constellations in the region of the ecliptic are associated with the astrological signs of the zodiac. The zodiac is a band centred on the ecliptic. Although the constellations have no clear boundaries, the signs are regarded as occupying equal fractions of the ecliptic and, as there are twelve of them, each corresponds to 30 degrees of the circle (there being 360 degrees in the whole circle).

In order to identify the positions of the signs precisely, a starting-point is needed. Convenient marks are supplied by the equinoctial points. Twice a year at the equinoxes the periods of day and night are equal. This occurs on about 21 March and 21 September. These times are mid-way between the time of midsummer (the longest day) and midwinter (the shortest day). At the vernal equinox in March, the position of the Sun in the zodiac is called the 0th degree of the first sign. As the signs are arranged on a circle there is no 'first sign' but conventionally the order is as listed below.

Aries	Libra
Taurus	Scorpio
Gemini	Sagittarius
Cancer	Capricorn
Leo	Aquarius
Virgo	Pisces

The zodiac defined above is referred to as the 'tropical zodiac'.

There is an astrological school which prefers a 'sidereal zodiac' which is one where 0 degrees Aries is defined by reference to the fixed stars. The two zodiacs slowly separate over millennia because of a phenomenon known as the precession of the equinoxes. The precession corresponds to the wobble of a spinning top. One complete wobble rotation of the earth takes 26,000 years and one zodiac moves 360 degrees relative to the other during that time. Thus the separation is about one sign per 2,000 years and the two zodiacs are currently approaching one sign apart. This means that the two schools associated with their respective zodiacs will usually give different interpretations of the same horoscope (because the meanings of the signs in the two zodiacs are kept much the same). One would expect that experience would show clearly which zodiac should be preferred, but no rapprochement between the schools has yet occurred. The majority of practising astrologers use the tropical zodiac.

The zodiac, Sun, Moon and planets provide the first set of factors for reading the horoscope. A planet is considered to be associated with particular qualities and the sign in which it occurs modifies those qualities. Astrological textbooks offer lists of terms for defining each planetary quality but for a quick appreciation only single key words are listed below:

Sun	self-expression
Moon	response
Mercury	communication
Venus	harmony
Mars	energy
Jupiter	expansion
Saturn	limitation
Uranus	change
Neptune	nebulousness
Pluto	renewal

Interpretation is done by considering the modification introduced by the sign in which a planet occurs. Thus the modification generated by Aries is (in terms of adverbs): assertively, energetically, aggressively. If a horoscope shows the Sun in Aries it implies that the self-expression will be assertive, energetic and aggressive (though influenced by other factors which will be present).

The position of the Sun in the horoscope is the basis of 'newspaper astrology' because the Sun's sign position is easily ascertained from the birthday to within a degree or two. The Sun spends roughly a month in each of the twelve signs, entering a fresh sign on about the 21st of each month. To discover the whereabouts of the Moon and each planet requires a special calendar called an ephemeris which lists the positions in the zodiac of each of those bodies. Using the appropriate ephemeris for the year of birth one can look up the day and read off the sign and degree of that sign for each of the planets. The Moon moves through the signs much faster than any of the planets and it is necessary to take into account the hour as well as the day of birth to obtain the Moon's position. It can be seen that the complexity of the horoscope greatly exceeds that obtained from the Sun sign alone. There are an additional nine planetary factors, each one modified by the sign in which it occurs.

The pattern of the heavens is much the same all day long. The Sun travels about a degree a day and the planets usually more slowly than that. Only the Moon shifts appreciably because it moves through all twelve signs during its phases, corresponding to about one sign every two and a half days or about 12 degrees a day. However, the view of the pattern from earth changes hour by hour. In the same way that the Sun rises, reaches its zenith and sets, so each of the planets and the Moon does likewise. These effects derive from the rotation of the earth, which is quite separate from the motions of the planets through the signs. Each planet's apparent trajectory across the sky can take place during the day or the night, depending on the time of the year and current sign position of the planet, but it is only visible when it is above the horizon at night. Because planets have magnitude (equivalent to visibility) comparable with the visible stars they are completely outshone by the Sun and cannot be seen by day.

From the astrological point of view a planet is particularly important if it is rising, i.e. close to the horizon, or culminating, i.e. close to its zenith or highest point reached above the horizon. All other possible positions of a planet, between rising and culminating, between culminating and setting and below the horizon are associated with specific areas of activity. In fact the circle is divided into twelve just as for the signs, but this time the separate arcs are called 'houses'. The 1st house lies immediately below the horizon and houses two to six carry on below the horizon up to the Descendant — or setting point. Houses seven to twelve fill the circle above the horizon.

Each house corresponds to a specific area of activity:

1. The person
2. Possessions, feelings
3. Communications
4. Home
5. Creative, love, children
6. Service
7. Partners
8. Sex, death, inheritance
9. Travel, study
10. Public standing
11. Objectives, group involvement
12. Sacrifice, escape

Thus a planet appearing in a sign and in a house will indicate a quality, suitably modified and operating in a particular area of life. For example, the Sun in Aries in the 9th house suggests a personality in which vitality appears assertively in the area of travel and study. One might sum that up as 'a bold traveller'.

Opinions differ on how the house boundaries should be set. Methods of house division are named after past astrologers who devised them. For example, Placidus and Regiomontanus devised the Placidean and Regiomontanian systems respectively. There is no theoretical basis for preferring a particular house system and no clear consensus has emerged based on experience. However there is the merit of simplicity to recommend the 'Equal House system' which, as its name implies, requires each house to occupy 30 degrees starting at the rising point or Ascendant with the first and proceeding round the 360 degrees of the circle.

We have now covered enough points to study the horoscope or birth chart itself and an example is shown in Figure 1. It has been constructed for someone born at 6.00 a.m. on 20 February 1928

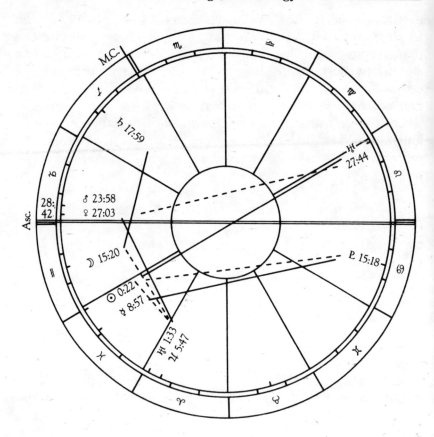

Figure 1 *Horoscope or natal chart for someone born at 6.00 a.m. on 20 February 1928 at Bournemouth, England.*

at Bournemouth, England. The rising point is 28 degrees of Capricorn. This has been found from the 1928 ephemeris by noting the sidereal time at noon on 20 February and correcting back 6 hours to yield 15 hours 55 minutes 44 seconds, which corresponds to 28:42 of Capricorn. Sidereal time is measured relative to the fixed stars, in contrast with solar time which is measured relative to the Sun. The earth rotates 365¼ times relative to the Sun in one year, but it has itself circled the Sun once during that same year and has completed 366¼ rotations relative to the fixed stars. Thus the sidereal day is a little shorter than the solar day — nearly 4 minutes shorter. Hence the relationship between GMT and sidereal time is quite complicated (not least because every four years we introduce an extra day as 29 February to allow for the quarter rotation which the Sun makes in addition to its 365 rotations for a whole year — and thereby avoid a steady drift of the equinoxes through the calendar). It should be apparent from these complications why an ephemeris is needed to calculate the rising point. Bournemouth is close enough in longitude to London (for which the ephemeris has been compiled) so no correction for longitude was needed. For births at places which are substantially east or west of London a longitude correction (15 degrees of longitude equivalent to one hour) is required to find the sidereal time at birth.

Shown on the birth chart is the MC, which stands for *Medium Coeli* or Midheaven — this is the point of the ecliptic which is culminating and it is also obtained from the ephemeris. The signs and the planets are shown by their symbols to avoid clutter on the chart. To facilitate reading the chart, a check-list is provided below:

♈	Aries	☉	Sun
♉	Taurus	☽	Moon
♊	Gemini	☿	Mercury
♋	Cancer	♀	Venus
♌	Leo	♂	Mars
♍	Virgo	♃	Jupiter
♎	Libra	♄	Saturn
♏	Scorpio	♅	Uranus
♐	Sagittarius	♆	Neptune
♑	Capricorn	♇	Pluto
♒	Aquarius		
♓	Pisces		

Because the houses follow round consecutively, they are not numbered. It can be readily seen that Moon is in the 1st house, Sun and Mercury are in the 2nd, Pluto in the 6th, Neptune in the 7th, Saturn in the 11th and Mars and Venus in the 12th.

There are lines drawn connecting certain planets. These are to indicate the 'aspects' which are particular angular relationships between points on the ecliptic. Two planets which are very close are said to be in 'conjunction' (Mars/Venus and Jupiter/Uranus are conjunctions in the example chart). Two planets close to 180 degrees separation are spoken of as being in 'opposition' (Sun/Neptune are in opposition in the chart). Two planets separated by 120 degrees are in 'trine' (Mercury/Pluto make a weak trine in the chart). If the separation is 90 degrees then it is a 'square' (there are no squares in the chart). A 60 degree separation is a 'sextile' and there are some minor aspects: 150 degrees 'quincunx', 30 degrees 'semi-sextile', 45 degrees 'semi-square', 135 degrees 'sesquiquadrate', 72 degrees 'quintile' and 144 degrees 'bi-quintile'.

An aspect between two planets is considered to enhance the qualities associated with those planets but in specific ways that depend on the type of aspect. The conjunction adds to the joint strength, the trine (and to a lesser extent the sextile) generates harmonious working between the two planets, whilst the opposition implies strain and the square indicates difficulty. The remainder of the aspects, except for the quintile, relate to minor difficulty. Aspects are, in general, not exact and an 'orb' is allowed. For the major aspects (conjunction, opposition, trine and square) up to about 8 degrees either way is allowed. For the minor aspects only half this orb is allowable and for both major and minor aspects the strength is considered to fall away sharply as the separation increases from exactness.

Interpretation of the Horoscope

Among astrologers, the emphasis on features which are important varies considerably — for some practitioners, there are more arcane points to watch than have been listed in this 'mainline' survey. For example, the shape of the overall planetary distribution is sometimes thought to matter. In the example chart all the planets except Neptune and Pluto cluster within 110 degrees in the neighbourhood of the rising point. This might suggest a highly self-centred individual for whom family, partners and public life are all secondary considerations.

'Rulership' is a further factor to note. Each planet is considered to have an affinity with a particular sign or pair of signs and the ruler of the rising sign has a special import in the chart. For example, Venus rules Taurus and Libra, so for charts with either of these signs rising, the position of Venus and the aspects it makes with other planets would merit attention. In the example chart

Capricorn is rising; the ruler of Capricorn is Saturn, which here is in Sagittarius in the eleventh house with only a sextile to the Moon. This would suggest a serious practical disposition expressed through interests and objectives.

All aspects in the chart are to be studied, with the major ones given the most emphasis. Thus, in the example chart the most important aspect is an opposition between the Sun and Neptune within 3 degrees of exactitude and occurring between the 2nd and 8th houses. One could expect the feelings and emotions of this individual to be infused with a strong element of idealism.

Rulership and aspects belong to the 'main theme', but there are a number of variations. For some there are symbolic meanings associated with every one of the 360 degrees and the occupancy of particular degrees is deemed important. Less comprehensively but probably with more experience to support it is the concept of 'degree areas' — small arcs in particular signs whose occupancy is significant. Some astrologers consider the Moon's Nodes to be important. In astronomical terms, a planet's nodes are the two points where its orbit intersects the plane of the ecliptic. The Moon's Nodes are not in fact marked in the example chart and some might regard that as a serious omission.

It would be merely confusing to add to the list of items above and they were mentioned only to convey the flavour of a variety of possibilities available for use in interpretation. The situation is something like the coexistence of schools of psychotherapists all seeking the same goal but favouring significantly different approaches. This resemblance is even closer because practitioners in both areas tend to develop very personal styles.

It would be wrong, however, to convey the impression that astrological practice is riven by schism and hopelessly fragmented. There is a main stream whose principal features were listed earlier (the signs, planets, angles, houses and aspects). For example it would be surprising if any professional astrologer failed to notice a central paradox in the example chart. Mars conjunct Venus signifies emotions easily aroused and the conjunction is almost exactly on the Ascendant; yet it occurs in a sign — Capricorn — which is, above all the signs, cool, calculating and aloof!

The Evidence

The brief account of astrological tenets given above derives from mainstream European practice (there are considerable differences between European and Hindu astrology) with the modern period dating from Alan Leo (1860-1917). Leo wrote thirty books on astrology and his teachings spread world-wide. Subsequent textbooks have drawn on Leo's work, modified by published research and by the experience of the authors. Clearly, what is needed is an appreciation of the evidence for the soundness of the material appearing in those textbooks. What follows is a short survey of the main evidence relating to traditional astrology drawing primarily on well-documented studies and omitting work which is lacking in some respect (usually replication). There is no attempt to be comprehensive and to some extent the choice reflects the author's personal taste.

Astrological consultants who have many clients and have looked at large numbers of charts necessarily come to hold strong views about the importance of particular significators. If challenged on a point they are likely to respond: 'It works for me.' The difficulty with statements derived from personal chart collections is that a small cluster of instances provokes interest and anticipation of discovering a 'rule'. Thereafter the tendency to seek confirming instances grows. If a disconfirming case crops up then there is a temptation to 'explain it away' by some special factor which was present. People vary greatly in their inclination and capacity to remain disinterested and impartial when judging an apparent correlation. Furthermore there can be difficulty in assessing how likely it is that an apparent correlation could arise by chance, unless the assessor has some knowlege of statistics. In other fields, such as medicine, the use of large collections of cases analysed by statistical methods has become routine. Although a doctor is quite likely to defend a statement about a prognosis by saying: 'In my experience . . .', if he is challenged, he would certainly wish to cite a clinical trial, the results of which had been published in a reputable journal. However, statistical methods have entered astrology to only a small extent and the proportion of astrologers who attempt statistical tests is still tiny. The reason for this is the widespread view that the horoscope, like the individual, is an organic unity. The various factors contributing to the whole personality are indissolubly linked and it is the whole chart that must be judged. This view has a close parallel with that of practitioners of holistic medicine who deprecate the orthodox style of associating disease with malfunctioning of specific organs and instead aim at treating the whole person. Though this gestalt approach is appealing, it makes progress in building up a set of well-established rules very difficult. A more balanced way could lie in accepting a role for both approaches. Statistical methods are possible in astrology and, as shown later, can lead to new insights, but the gestalt method is equally important. Indeed, all fields of science contain examples of vividly new relationships appearing because a researcher had an overwhelming sense of the underlying organic unity of the cosmos. Michael Faraday sought a connection between magnetism and light despite the lack of any hint that such a link existed. He looked because he believed that the various physical fluxes were all part of a total integrated structure. He was in fact rewarded by discovering rotation of the plane of polarized light by a magnetic field. This ability to glimpse the whole is a remarkable human faculty and one to be cherished. It seems unlikely that any forays into the field of so-called artificial intelligence will get anywhere near it.

In order to preserve the whole picture, i.e. to meet the requirement for retaining the whole chart, a special kind of statistical test for astrological powers of character delineation was devised. Given a group of individuals, one can present the astrologer with a set of horoscopes, each of which refers to one of the group and also a set of character descriptions, each of which again refers to one of the group. The astrologer's task is to match each horoscope with its corresponding character description. Even if the astrologer fails to get every pairing right, the probability of any specific score between zero and all correct can be readily calculated. For example if a group of ten individuals were used the probabilities of obtaining 0, 1, 2, 3, etc., up to 10 pairings correct are as follows:

Correct pairings	Probability
0	0.37
1	0.63

Correct pairings	Probability
2	0.26
3	0.08
4	0.02
5	0.004
6	0.0005
7	0.00008
8	0.00001
10	0.0000003

The chance of getting at least one right is better than evens and of getting three right is only 11 to 1 against. It is necessary to score at least 4 to be interesting — but if anyone got them all right that would be a one in 4 million chance. Such tests have been performed a number of times, the most celebrated being those of the American astrologer Vernon Clark.[2] Clark published results which were well above chance level and which suggested that, indeed, astrologers can often accurately divine character from a horoscope. However, there is a problem if the tester, i.e. the one who selects the individuals to be included in the group, is himself an astrologer, because he will tend to select subjects whose charts do conform with their characters. There is no need to ascribe any fraudulent intention; such special choices could take place quite unwittingly. In order for the tests to be unbiased the selection of individuals would have to be made by a non-astrologer or better still using a random method of selection.

Gauquelin[3] has described a variation of the matching test which he himself has set for astrologers to attempt. His variation is to provide twenty horoscopes, ten of which are for individuals with some marked trait and the other ten for individuals with the opposite trait, e.g. ten criminals with ten law-abiding persons, ten mentally ill with ten sane, etc. The astrologer is required to distinguish the two groups using only the charts. Gauquelin reports that though this test has been performed several times, the astrologers obtain only chance level scores.

It can be stated that tests of astrology making use of the whole chart as a means of identification, where the test design has been such as to avoid the possibility of bias, have not yielded results above chance level. This is a severe blow to traditional astrology and it is not easy to provide a satisfactory explanation. The following suppositions are possible:

1. The current rules of astrological interpretation are defective, possibly because they have been corrupted over the centuries.

2. The current generation of astrologers lacks the ability to generate successful syntheses from the chart factors.

3. The details which are supplied about the individuals who make up the test groups, though they refer to physical appearance, character traits, interests, profession, etc., do not necessarily cover the potential which is present. For example, a woman may have the potential to be an artist, yet spend her active years as a wife and mother.

4. Astrology may apply only to certain individuals and the fraction of the test group to whom it applies may not be large enough for the test results to be convincing.

Most astrologers would reject all these possible explanations except for number 3. It is a part of astrological tradition that the chart refers to potential, not all of which may be actualized. As with any branch of science, the appropriate step when faced with a choice of possible explanations is to devise experiments whose outcomes will lend weight to one or other of them. Some sorts of explanation are difficult to test and number 3 comes into that class. If a variable but unknown proportion of potential is actualized, this provides a very elastic sort of explanation that can be stretched to fit almost any disparity between a chart and the person to whom it applies. However, this does not mean that all avenues of investigation are blocked. There are many ways of detecting possible relationships between celestial patterns and human life. One method to which reference has already been made is that of using collections of individuals who all share the same attribute or alternatively who all have the same significator in their charts.

Statistical Tests

Much effort has been expended to demonstrate the validity of the

'Sun signs', i.e. a correlation between the sign which the Sun occupied at birth and the character or profession or appearance of the corresponding group of individuals. One of the reasons for the interest in this particular part of astrology is the ease with which the Sun sign can be ascertained (roughly speaking, only the month and the day within that month of the birthday is needed).

However, there are pitfalls in astrological testing. One of the more subtle is self-attribution. Mayo,[4] in collaboration with White and Eysenck, designed a test using a questionnaire which was completed by 2,000 people. It was a questionnaire to elicit psychological factors and from it could be deduced an extroversion/introversion score. The score was checked against the occurrence of the Sun in those signs traditionally linked with masculine, positive attributes (and extroversion) — Aries, Gemini, Leo, Libra, Sagittarius and Aquarius. Similarly the check was made for those signs linked with feminie, negative attributes (and introversion) — Taurus, Cancer, Virgo, Scorpio, Capricorn and Pisces. The association of extroverts with positive signs and introverts with negative signs was statistically strong and the publication of the results aroused considerable interest. But when Gauquelin attempted a replication of the experiment in France, he found no trace of the association. This suggests that the conditions of the Mayo test may have contained bias of some kind. It emerged that Mayo's subjects were mainly students of astrology who were already aware of the interpretations placed on the Sun signs. Thus they would tend to respond to the questions in the light of interpretations attaching to their own personal Sun signs.

One of the great advantages of the statistical approach is that it is often possible, by the exercise of ingenuity, to devise a variation of the experiment which will yield the answer to a 'supplementary question'. The original question was: 'Is there an association between Sun signs and extroversion/introversion?' The supplementary question is: 'Could this association arise from self-attribution and therefore be spurious?' The ingenious device in this instance was to break the test population into three groups:

1. experienced students, well versed in all branches of astrology;
2. those knowing only the signs of the zodiac;

3.   those with no knowledge of astrology.

Eysenck[5] reported the result of checks on the degree of association found for each of these groups. The significant level of association persisted only for the second group. The plausible explanation for this finding is that those with no knowledge of the traditional interpretations would not bias the outcome. Similarly, those experienced students, aware of many other factors in the chart, would not be unduly influenced by Sun signs. However, those for whom astrology was largely the Sun signs and their qualities would tend towards self-attribution and bias their answers to the questionnaire.

This account was preceded by the caveat that it was intended as a 'plausible explanation' and it would be unsound to make a stronger statement unless there were corroborative evidence, though it should be mentioned that Pawlik and Buse[6] have demonstrated the same tendency for people, knowing their Sun signs, to bias answers to personality assessment questionnaires.

The effect of personal bias, either self-bias or that of an assessor, can be reduced if the attributes of the subjects are derived from an objective source, say the profession of the subject. The choice of profession that a subject makes may, it is true, have been influenced by the knowledge of what professions are traditionally associated with the Sun sign but it is doubtful if this possible connection actually exists. First, because Sun sign and profession appear to be very weakly related if at all, and secondly because other factors concerning the diurnal circle, do emerge as highly significant — and the pattern in the subject's diurnal circle is only rarely known to him. Finally, even when the diurnal pattern is known to the subject, the traditional interpretation would steer him away from the association found empirically. This last point is relevant to an argument appearing in the *Biologist*[7] a few years ago attempting to explain away the Gauquelin results as due to a form of self-attribution. The author suggested that a mother-to-be would be concerned that her child be born at an auspicious time, i.e. with a planet 'well placed' in the diurnal circle and this could influence birth time, or even recording of the birth time. This hypothesis falls down when it is appreciated that the Gauquelin auspicious planetary areas do not coincide with the traditional ones, so that even if the first requirements for the hypothesis to be met were present (parental knowledge of the traditional planetary influence in relationship to the angles and knowledge of the current positions of the planets in the sky) this would not provide a means of amplifying the Gauquelin effect.

Given data which are free from bias there are further snares to avoid in statistical work. Bias by the assessor or by the subject himself has bedevilled the work of Clark and Mayo. The next problem concerns sample size. The collection of data is laborious and it is tempting to draw conclusions from a handful of charts because the odds against a particular finding being due to chance appear to be overwhelming. Furthermore, there are insurmountable difficulties in extending certain collections. If you want to study presidents of the United States or winners of the Miss World contest then you must make do with only a small collection.

Charles Carter,[8] who was one of the most important figures in twentieth-century astrology, often quoted research results based on only a score or two of charts. I recall his liking the argument that modest samples, in spite of their paucity, could nevertheless be highly significant. He remarked on one occasion that if a die were thrown and came down uppermost on six successive throws you could be sure that it was loaded. The odds are indeed nearly 50,000 to 1 against its happening — and his assertion was an entirely reasonable one. However, the mathematics of solar distribution statistics is not as straightforward as raising 6 to the power of 6, and unless a distribution is highly non-uniform one needs quite a large sample to demonstrate statistical significance. This point has not been appreciated by most of those who draw conclusions from modest collections of data. It is worth demonstrating with an example.

Suppose a researcher has a collection of 100 charts of people in profession X. One could expect about 100/12 or 8.5 for each of the Sun signs. The expectancy per sign is not precisely that figure because the earth's angular velocity round the Sun is not constant and also there is a natural preponderance of births in the spring months, but for this purpose these are minor details. Suppose that the distribution is as shown opposite.

♈	♉	♊	♋	♌	♍	♎	♏	♐	♑	♒	♓
16	5	8	9	8	7	10	6	8	7	9	7

Nearly double the average expectancy occurs in Aries; surely this is significant? Well for the straightforward question: 'What is the probability of taking a sample of 100 and getting 16 in Aries?' the answer is more than 100 to 1 against and a researcher who made this calculation would feel justified in considering that the distribution is telling us something meaningful about profession X. But the proper question is: 'What is the probability of getting this particular distribution?' (remembering that very low figures are unlikely, as well as very high figures). There is an appropriate statistical test termed the chi square test and for this distribution it yields a chi square value of 10 which for 11 degrees of freedom (one less than the number of signs) is quite unremarkable. One could expect to get that sort of chi square value for most of the results if one carried out an experiment allocating 100 items randomly among 12 boxes each with equal probability.

The effect of sample size is important. If exactly the same proportions had occurred with a sample of 300, i.e. 48 in Aries, 15 in Taurus, etc., then the chi square value would have been 30 and that figure is highly significant — 1,000 to 1 against its arising by chance. Using suitably sized samples, the expectancy must be calculated with care. This means taking the frequency with which each Sun sign is represented in the general population. Because there is a preponderance of spring births, the above-average level of Sun in Aries is less significant than the elementary calculation reveals (Sun in Aries covers the last third of March and most of April). There is a further requirement. To be confident that a result is meaningful it is necessary to replicate it: to obtain a sample from another source and show that the same pattern is again generated. This procedure is necessary because the initial sample may be biased in some way unknown to the researcher, and the chance of this same bias occurring in a second sample, especially if drawn from a separate population, is remote.

Sun Position

Recalling that position of the Sun in the chart has been

traditionally considered an important astrological factor, one might have expected that some collections, particularly the large ones, would have yielded impressive results. In spite of numerous studies, the outcome has been disappointing. Dean[9] lists over sixty collections including musicians, clergymen, doctors, bankers, soldiers, idiots, politicians, boxers, psychiatrists and businessmen. The number in each collection was usually in the thousands and for a few collections over ten thousand. Only one or two of the collections show uneven Sun sign occupancy to the point of statistical significance, and of course if there are many separate collections it can be expected that a small fraction of them will be unusual, in the same way that a surprisingly large total may appear in one sign — just because there are twelve opportunities for it to occur.

If the Sun sign is important then most of these collections should have demonstrated it with high levels of significance. With a sample of thousands even a few per cent departure from expected levels becomes overwhelmingly unlikely. In fact, the percentage deviations in these collections were minuscule. How can this repeated failure be explained? The following suppositions are possible:

1. The sign position of the Sun in the chart does matter but to a much lesser extent than tradition indicates.
2. The tropical zodiac is wrong and some form of sidereal zodiac should be used.
3. The relationship between Sun and other elements (planets, angles or nodes making aspects with the Sun) is what matters rather than signs.
4. The position of the Sun in the diurnal circle, i.e. the house it occupies, is the critical factor.
5. It is neither sign nor house that is important but some other feature such as a set of potent degree areas.

There may be some support for the first supposition. The work of Smithers,[10] using very large samples obtained by computer search from a national database, indicates that some results, e.g. for secretaries as an occupational class, do replicate successfully and reach acceptable significance levels though the percentage deviations from chance expectancies were small.

With regard to the second supposition, Bradley[11] attempted a search for the 'best zodiac' using a sample of nearly 2,500 US clergymen. By starting at 0 Aries, 1 Aries, 2 Aries, etc., up to 29 Aries, he was able to list the Sun distribution in thirty separate zodiacs. Each one was checked for the overall chi square value in order to find the maximum — which would indicate a 'best zodiac'. In fact, the values revealed a flat peak with no really clear point as maximum. The position of the peak did lend support to one favoured sidereal zodiac and Bradley took this as proof of the validity of that zodiac. It was not entirely convincing — there was no replication and other attempts to find whether a tropical or a sidereal zodiac best fits the data have been similarly unconvincing.

The third supposition is an awkward one to check because the apparent movement of a planet is far from simple. Daily observation of the exterior planets (those with orbital radii greater than the earth's) shows that each at some time undergoes 'retrograde motion', i.e. it pauses in its path, becomes stationary and back-tracks for a little way before resuming its orginal forward movement. The explanation for this effect lies in the fact that the observer, being terrestrially based, is moving and that movement affects all observations. The change of position of a planet which we see is a change relative to the fixed stars. If we, travelling in the same direction as the planet, 'go past' it then it will appear to be going backwards relative to the fixed stars. The same effect is also observed for the interior planets (Mercury and Venus) but is less easily noted because their angular distance from the Sun remains small, which means that they are only visible for short periods after sunset or in the morning before sunrise.

Because of retrograde motion, the time that a planet is aspected by the Sun depends on the period being studied. For example, if a planet is retrograde as the Sun comes into aspect with it, the time during which the aspect applies will be shorter than if the planet had maintained forward motion. One means of overcoming the problem of this unsystematic variability is to take a control from randomly selected people covering the same segment of time as the test group and compare the occurrence of aspects in the test group against those in the control. Dieschbourg[12] used this technique on a number of chart collections and found that aspects between Sun and Jupiter appeared 20 per cent more often for military leaders than for the controls. Although the sample was only 170, this is significant (500 to 1 against). He also found 17 per cent more Sun/Neptune aspects for a sample of 915 philosophers/historians, which is highly significant (more than 2,000 to 1 against).

For the fourth proposition, there is the extensive and detailed work of Gauquelin[13] to draw upon. Although he found that the position of a planet in the diurnal circle does matter for Venus, Mars, Jupiter, Saturn and the Moon, the frequencies for the Sun, Mercury and outer planets (Uranus, Neptune and Pluto) were not different from chance levels.

Finally, for the last supposition that it is neither sign nor house which is important, there is a concept arising only in the modern era. This is the idea that the occurrence of a planet in the zodiac drawn from a special collection of charts is not well described by a set of parcels each 30 degrees long, but rather by a smoothly changing wave pattern. The idea was broached by Krafft[14] but was independently developed and refined by Addey[15] and the author. Analysis of distributions to find the wave content is described in Chapter 3. Here it is noted that the analysis applied to the distribution of the Sun in collections of poliomyelitis victims and clergymen does indicate that certain waves are prominent.

This brief survey of the evidence for the Sun's astrological importance suggests that in spite of great efforts to vindicate 'Sun signs' there is little evidence of anything but a very weak effect. Similarly, the position of the Sun in the diurnal circle does not seem to have any detectable influence. Solar aspects to the planets look more promising and there may well be a different form for solar influence via wave effects.

Houses and Planetary Aspects

There are two remaining facets of traditional astrology that have been examined statistically. The first concerns planetary occupancy of the houses. The variety of house systems that have been devised has already been mentioned earlier. That due to Placidus is probably the most widely used apart from the equal house system. Gauquelin's method of dividing the diurnal circle corresponds quite closely to Placidean house division and he checked large collections (of the order of 1,000 for each sample) for appropriate house occupancy. For example, one should expect from traditional teaching that artists would have the 5th house occupied because this is the house associated with creative and artistic work, but the charts of over 900 painters revealed only chance levels of occupancy for Sun, Moon, Mercury, Venus, Jupiter and Saturn. Similarly for other collections such as writers (the 3rd house) and criminals (the 12th house) the occupancy levels were unremarkable. The interesting point about the houses is that Gauquelin's research in the diurnal circle has demonstrated in effect that those houses traditionally regarded as weak and referred to as 'cadent' (numbers 12, 3, 6 and 9) correspond approximately to the sectors of the diurnal circle which show higher planetary occupancy than chance levels. A detailed account of this research is given in the next chapter.

The second topic of interest is that of aspects among planets other than the Sun. Solar aspects have already received mention in connection with the work of Dieschbourg. He has also investigated non-solar aspects in the charts of numerous collections of professionals. Some of his results are quite striking. Mercury/Uranus aspects in the charts of nearly 2,000 writers are above expected levels to an extent which would occur by chance only once in 10,000 times. Similarly, Venus/Saturn for 500 painters and sculptors, and Mars/Jupiter for 1,000 scientists are both at levels approaching 1,000 to 1 against their arising by chance. Although Dieschbourg looked at many interplanetary aspects and could therefore have expected to find a few unusual results, the ones quoted above are at such high significance levels that they stand in their own right. It is a pity that he did not attempt replication experiments because successful replication adds substantially to the quality of the evidence.

What is interesting about these findings is that, in large measure, they accord with the accepted meanings that are associated with the planets. Thus Mercury, planet of communication, in aspect with Uranus for originality, should be found in the charts of writers. Venus, planet of beauty, joined with Saturn for form and structure, should occur in the horoscopes of sculptors. Neptune, planet of mysticism and philosophy, unsurprisingly turns up in the charts of philosophers. Mars/Jupiter aspects in the charts of scientists is not something that would have been expected from traditional teachings. It is not wholly inappropriate, but other planets, particularly Saturn, would have been expected to be prominent.

These findings parallel those of Gauquelin, to be considered shortly, in that traditional meanings of the planets are confirmed. The 'new astrology' is a tantalizing selection from the old, accompanied by surprises of recent vintage. The signs and the traditional houses get no support, but the planetary qualities are corroborated and there is evidence for the aspects. It may be that the aspects are an emergent effect of the wave patterns which were mentioned earlier, and this point will be taken up later when the waves are considered in detail.

2
THE GAUQUELIN RESEARCH

Michel and Françoise Gauquelin

Michel Gauquelin trained as a statistician and although having an early interest in astrology he is, above all else, an empiricist. He can say in company with Bertrand Russell that he is unwilling to believe anything unless there is evidence for its being true. This is a stark, unyielding position which is found only rarely among people at large, and very rarely among astrologers. To practise astrology requires the acceptance of many tenets for which little or no evidence is offered in the textbooks. It is therefore all the more remarkable that a man with such an innately sceptical temperament should undertake tests to establish the truth or otherwise of astrology. It is quite extraordinary that, having found traditional astrology to show up very poorly when applied to his early collections, he went on to pursue his own investigations of planetary correlation and profession with relentless application.

He had started on his search for suitable data before marrying and his wife Françoise encouraged and assisted him. To secure copies of the birth certificates of particular individuals often entails visits to the local offices where records are kept and this can absorb much time when the object is to build large collections. For this labour alone the Gauquelins would merit a place in astrological annals. In the early years of their work they carried out all the searches and the compilations themselves. More recently there has been assistance from students and from computing specialists who were able to store all the original data on files and perform checks of the calculations that had previously been performed manually.

Choice of Data

One of the difficulties facing anyone attempting an investigation of astrology is that many of the traditional chart indications refer to psychological characteristics and the actual manifestation of such traits is considered as a possibility rather than an inevitable consequence. Thus a Capricornian meriting the label of one with a taste for order and structure would not necessarily show this trait by taking up a career as a crystallographer. Even if crystallography did loom, it might only be during some short period of his life. Traits are notoriously difficult to pin down. People are not good at self-analysis, nor is there a consistent, reliable personality for the investigator to measure. For example, a person may be impetuous on one day and cautious the next.

A possible way of reducing this difficulty is to choose only those people who are extreme in some sense — approaching a 'pure type'. Additionally the choice could be restricted to people who have consistently followed some vocation or profession, because this would show an underlying strong propensity rather than some ephemeral characteristic. Gauquelin used this approach in his collections of data. For example, one of his early collections was of notorious criminals. In order to provide a wide base he sought the birth data of those in many distinctive professions such as physician, writer and musician; also of people distinguished by their eminence in some pursuit such as athletics or politics. Not only did this method approach the ideal of the 'pure type' but it also enabled him to put a quantitative measure on the degree of eminence reached by the members of his collections. Thus an athlete who represented his or her country in Olympic events is to be considered more eminent than one whose prestige is only at the national or regional level.

The Findings

The astrological researcher does not start with a blank sheet. There have been other workers in the field. Some using statistical methods have claimed vindication for parts of the traditional teachings. For example Choisnard[1] and Krafft[2] had both claimed that a sort of astral heredity existed with children tending to share the sign position of specific planets with their parents. It is necessary to be very careful in drawing conclusions from statistics and Gauquelin was able to show that Choisnard and Krafft had failed to make allowance for demographic effects and that their results were without significance. He himself searched for any evidence in his own collections of a tendency for particular signs to have above-average occupancies or for specific aspects to be over-represented. On neither of these points was there anything of significance to report. It was only when he examined the occurrence of planets in the diurnal circle that remarkable distributions came to light. The position of a planet in the diurnal circle corresponds to what astrologers refer to as 'house position'. A brief mention of houses and their place in astrology was made in the first chapter. If a planet is about to rise, i.e. to appear above the horizon, it is in the 1st house. If it has just risen it is in the twelfth. The remaining ten houses are distributed round the circle in order. The actual boundaries between adjacent houses are determined in a variety of ways according to particular house systems. For the simplest scheme (the Equal House system) each house occupies 30 degrees of the ecliptic. More elaborate house systems (the so-called Quadrant systems) are designed to squeeze just three houses in the ecliptic interval between Ascendant and culminating point, three more between culminating point and Descendant and the remaining six below the horizon divided similarly between the two remaining quadrants. Gauquelin avoided use of any house system and determined the position of each planet simply by the time lapse from its passing the Ascendant or Descendant. The time lapse is then converted into an appropriate 'sector' by noting the fraction it makes of total time from Ascendant to Descendant. Thus, if a planet took 15 hours between rising and setting and the birth time occurred 7 hours after it had risen, the appropriate fraction would be $7/15$ and for a 36 sector division of the circle, the planet would be in the 9th sector because $(7 \div 15) \times 18 = 8.4$. In this calculation it is the fraction of 18 which is used because there are considered to be 18 sectors above the horizon and 18 sectors below it for a 36 sector division of the circle. The number 8.4 corresponds to the 9th sector because counting starts with the 1st sector rather than with the 0th sector (everything between 0 and 1 is in the first sector and everything between 8 and 9 is in the 9th sector). The number of sectors is chosen arbitrarily but clearly there is an advantage in avoiding too few because the distribution will then be coarse and show no fine detail. In contrast, if too many sectors are used the occupancy of each one will be so small that the distribution will appear 'noisy' because random effects will have been emphasized. Gauquelin has used sector divisions of 12, 18 and 36. Note that he counts the sectors in a clockwise direction from the Ascendant, whereas the houses of traditional astrology are counted anticlockwise from the Ascendant.

From an examination of the birth times of outstanding athletes it was found that their births occurred when Mars was present in those sectors close to the Ascendant and to the culminating point or MC much more often than in the other sectors. Similarly, this kind of pattern appeared for Saturn in the case of scientists and for Jupiter in the case of politicians. The pattern, in fact, repeated for a range of professions involving in each case 'appropriate' planets drawn from the group Mars, Jupiter, Saturn and the Moon. The appearance of a particular planet was appropriate in the sense that the traditional quality associated with that planet would be expected among members of the professional group where it was found. Thus Mars (martial qualities and energy) in the case of military leaders and athletes, but Saturn (order and structure) in the case of scientists.

Replications

When Gauquelin published his results for French professional groups, it was suggested by critics that the effects he had discovered could be purely local and confined to France. Although this may seem a rather curious and unlikely kind of criticism, there is still the requirement for replication of any such findings. In order to meet his critics, Gauquelin went on to repeat his collections of data in a set of European countries where birth times are usually recorded. The outcome of this immense labour was a set of profession birth time collections containing more than 15,000 individuals. The patterns he had found for the French data appeared just as strong for data drawn from Italy, Germany, Belgium and the Netherlands. Although the original results from France were statistically significant, the total collections reach extremely high

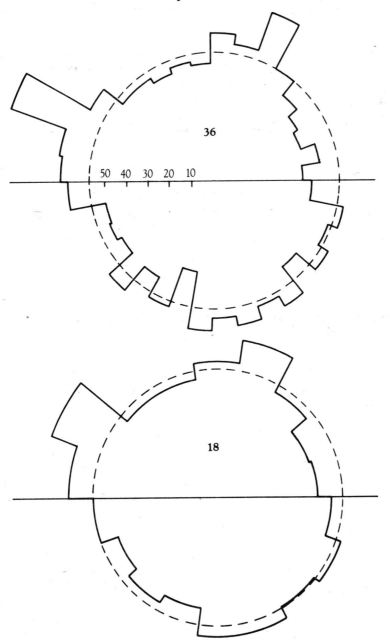

Figure 2 *Distribution of Mars in the charts of athletes for a 36-sector division and for an 18-sector division (from Gauquelin's data).*

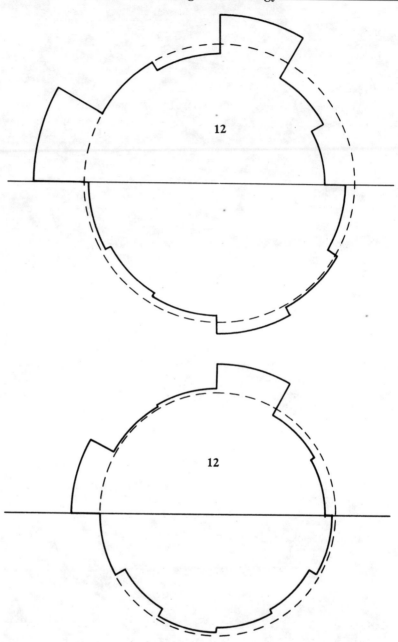

Figure 3 *Distributions (upper) of Mars in the charts of athletes and (lower) of Jupiter in the charts of military leaders (from Gauquelin's data).*

significance levels and could be expected by chance in only one of millions of trials.

The typical form of pattern found is shown in Figures 2 and 3, where the distribution of Mars at the birth times of athletes is illustrated for all of the European cases numbering in total 2,088. The data is shown for a 36-sector, an 18-sector and a 12-sector division of the circle. The radius of each sector has been made proportional to the number of cases found for that sector. For the first sector diagram, the number of expected cases (e.g. from a random population) is only slightly different from $2,088/36 = 58$. Exact calculation shows that the expected number varies from 62 in sector 2 to 54.6 in sector 20. The reason for these departures from a constant average value derives from the uneven distribution of births during each twenty-four hours (demographic factors) and the uneven distribution of Mars in the diurnal circle (astronomical factors).

The salient features of the distribution show up most obviously in the third diagram where only 12 sectors have been used. A surfeit of cases appears in the 1st and 4th sectors with modest departures from the mean in the remainder of the sectors. However, the most striking departures are seen in the first diagram, where the 3rd sector has 99 cases — over 60 per cent greater than is to be expected. This general type of pattern was observed separately for each country's data and for the pooled data. The pattern was seen for each professional group taken with its associated planet or planets, sometimes with two more minor peaks opposite the main ones, as in Figure 3 for Jupiter and military leaders. For a planet which is astrologically inappropriate to a given professional group the pattern is reversed, in the sense that the peaks immediately after the Ascendant and MC, characteristic of the diagrams considered above, are replaced by troughs.

Agreement with Astrology

One of the most intriguing features of the Gauquelin results is the agreement between prominence of a particular planet in the distribution for a professional group and the astrological appropriateness of that planet to the profession. This is shown in the following table:

Table 1

Professional group	Prominent planets
athletes	Mars
military leaders	Mars and Jupiter
scientists and physicians	Saturn and Mars
politicians	Jupiter and Moon
actors	Jupiter
writers	Jupiter and Moon

Conversely, there are lower than average frequencies seen in sectors immediately after the Ascendant and MC for certain planet and professional group combinations. This is shown in the table below:

Table 2

Professional group	Planets 'avoided'
athletes	Moon
military leaders	Moon
scientists and physicians	Jupiter
actors	Saturn
writers	Mars and Saturn
painters and musicians	Mars and Saturn

To have achieved even one of the results such as the Mars-athletes distribution would have been memorable; to obtain a whole set of such results with consistent agreement between astrological indicators and the corresponding professions is a monumental piece of work — a historic achievement.

Disagreement with Astrology

Of equal importance with the findings described above are the astrological indicators that Gauquelin failed to find. Although he examined the distributions of the other planets and of the Sun for each of his professional groups, he did not find departures from chance levels which were statistically significant. To the traditional astrologer this is disappointing. Why is Mercury not prominent in the case of writers and Neptune in the case of painters and musicians? Some evidence for the importance of Venus emerged when the search for personal characteristics was carried out, as described later in this chapter, but otherwise it is as if Sun, Mercury, Uranus, Neptune and Pluto were not there in the sky.

The second feature of the Gauquelin findings which is puzzling to traditional astrologers is the very fast fading of the patterns when the collections are widened to take in representatives of the groups who are in 'the second rank', i.e. of less than international stature. In the case of athletes, it means that fewer than one in 100,000 of the general population is eligible to be a member of the Gauquelin elite group, and if the selection includes 1 in 10,000 (corresponding to the top 0.01 per cent) then the prominence of Mars fades below statistical significance. Now this implies that if you think of the most outstanding athlete or sportsperson of your acquaintance whom you knew at school or college or whom you have met casually, then that individual is unlikely to be good enough for inclusion in the Gauquelin group. One might ask what use is astrological delineation if it fails to throw up an indication for the most extreme type you know — and what chance for the 'ordinary people' who by definition make up 99.99 per cent of the population?

The third feature of the results which contradicts traditional astrology is the location of the zones of importance in the chart. The Gauquelin zones correspond to the 9th and 12th houses, but these are traditionally the 'cadent' or weak houses of a chart. For example the 12th house is associated with retirement, escape, sacrifice and seclusion — certainly not the prominent life of the successful professional. The traditional houses are grouped as shown below:

Angular (implying powerful or initiatory)	houses 1,4,7,10
Succedent (implying resultant status)	houses 2,5,8,11
Cadent (implying dispersion)	houses 3,6,9,12

It is true to say that modern astrologers had tended to avoid calling the cadent houses 'weak' even before the Gauquelin work, but they would still have great difficulty in interpreting a 12th house Mars as indicative of military success — or even military leanings.

These three clear differences between the findings and traditional astrology have meant that most present-day astrologers are less than enthusiastic about Gauquelin. They welcome any research which contributes to the respectability of astrology as an empirical science but they do not want any of the traditional beliefs substantially amended — or, at the worst, overturned. However, there is one extension of the research which brings even greater concordance with traditional astrological canons and that is the work on personality traits described below.

Personality Traits

Although the strong associations between planetary position at birth time and professional success are impressive — and supportive of one facet from astrological lore — they say nothing about the types of people who become successful in the various professional fields. Even a cursory examination of the typical successful professional suggests that there are clear differences between the sort of person who is successful as a politician and one who achieves distinction in science. The question arises of whether the planets are indicative of profession or of those special personality features which are essential for professional success. It might seem at first sight that it would not be possible to disentangle the one effect from the other. If it is shown that athletes are active, daring, combative, etc., and that athletes tend to have Mars prominent at their birth times, it would not necessarily follow that there is any direct relationship between those qualities and the planet. Because young men drive sports cars and young men get involved in motor accidents (more often than women or older men) it does not follow that sports cars are inherently dangerous. However, if one is sufficiently ingenious in devising suitable experiments any underlying association can be extracted.

The problem of describing personality traits was noted earlier. It is unsatisfactory to ask people to describe themselves because the descriptions of an individual made by observers are found to differ markedly from that made by the individual himself. It would be unacceptable for the description of a subject's character traits to be made by the investigator because the likelihood of bias, even though entering unconsciously, is a serious risk. No critic of an experiment purporting to show an association between character-istics of individuals and planetary prominence would accept the outcome if the astrologer had written the descriptions of the individuals' characteristics. The way out of this difficulty is to take descriptions which have been made by independent observers for reasons that have nothing to do with astrology. Gauquelin used published biographies of his eminent subjects to obtain the descriptions he needed. In order to provide the necessary classi-fication of personal characteristics he extracted the adjectives which biographers had used in portraying their subjects. Thus if a biographer had spoken of his subject as 'fierce' or 'independent' or 'belligerent' then each of these words would be added to an inventory of personality traits in which the associated profession and the prominent planets would also be recorded. By this means it became possible to test several separate hypotheses.

The first hypothesis tested was that concerned with the planets indicating specific personality types which are expected in parti-cular professions. Gauquelin was able to show that if he took those athletes in his collection who were described as 'iron-willed' (an entirely appropriate term for an athlete) they showed Mars prominent twice as often as those athletes described as 'weak-willed'. Similar associations were found for other terms applicable to athletes and for other professional groups, each in relation to their own appropriate characteristics. For example writers spoken of as 'sensitive' appeared more often with Moon prominent than writers lacking this trait according to their biographers. In this way Gauquelin demonstrated that there was indeed a planet/charac-teristic association going beyond that which would follow merely from the known professional/characteristic association.

However, there is still a nagging doubt about these results, even though they carried high statistical significance. The distinctive groups identified by having a particular descriptor in common are still drawn from the same professional group. The surrounding aura of the profession is still there and it has not been shown that the planet/characteristic association occurs completely independ-ently of profession. In order to show this, it would be necessary to prove an association between planet and personality trait irrespective of the profession followed by the subject. Remarkably, Gauquelin was able to do this. Because the inventory of words alluding to traits had records of the prominent planets at the subject's birth time in each case he could discover which words appeared most frequently with each planet, independently of the profession involved in each case. By this means he could build up a 'planetary type' — a list of descriptors associated with each planet. Thus under Jupiter we find 'ambitious, conceited, independent, worldly . . .' under Saturn 'conscientious, discreet, meticulous, reserved . . .' under Mars 'active, brave, dynamic, reckless . . .' and under the Moon 'amiable, easy-going, imaginative, tolerant . . .' Furthermore he found that the antonyms of these descriptors (terms meaning the opposite, e.g. intolerant rather than tolerant) were associated with the absence of the appropriate planet from the regions of prominence.

These findings alone would be outstanding but there was an added bonus which truly crowns the achievement. Whereas Gauquelin had never been able to point to Venus as an indicator for a particular profession as he had done for Mars, Jupiter, Saturn and the Moon, he was able to discover what one may call 'the Venusian type'. He did this by the same technique of assembling those descriptors which were found to be associated with the planet in the prominent zones. Venus emerged with words such as: 'affable, attractive, charming, flattering, poetic . . .' This result is completely in accordance with the qualities with which traditional astrology has always invested Venus. Thus we have simultaneously a planetary/characteristic association emerging independently of the profession effect and a close concordance with the traditional meaning of the planet.

Ordinary People

The fast fading of the planet/profession effect as subjects of less professional acclaim are included has already been noted. It is not immediately obvious that there should be a comparable effect for personality traits. After all everyone knows acquaintances who exhibit one or more of the traits listed above and in some cases shows one of these traits to an extreme degree — so that all observers would agree so and so was very conscientious, or was extraordinarily charming, etc. It would seem quite natural therefore that one could set up an experiment demonstrating the planet/characteristic association for 'ordinary people'. Gauquelin has attempted this using various techniques for obtaining the necessary descriptions (substituting for the biographies which were available for his celebrities). In each of these trials the effects sought were weak or non-existent. This is a striking paradox. Gauquelin, with his usual honesty, reports his findings even though they appear discordant with the main body of his work. He finds it wellnigh incredible that the effects he has found for his elite groups do not apply in some measure to everyone else, and clearly if there is to be an explanation it will require concepts going beyond straightforward mechanistic interpretations. A possible interpretation is put forward in later chapters.

Heredity

During his work on the link between planetary position and profession, Gauquelin puzzled over the fact that the physical characteristics (and probably much of the personality) of a child are present in the foetus before it is born. He argued therefore that the planetary placing at birth corresponded to a timing effect rather than any direct influence which the planets might have on personality. Now the physical characteristics can to a large extent be traced to the genetic inheritance from the parents of the child and one could speculate further that some personality characteristics might also be inherited. It certainly appears that some inclinations and talents run in families. The Strauss family and the Bach family are good examples of musical talent apparently being inherited.

If personality characteristics are inherited and if these same characteristics are indicated by the planets which are prominent at the birth time, then one could expect some similarities between the prominent planets at the child's birth time and at the birth times of its parents. Traditional astrology has contained just such a belief in the form of expectations that the natal charts of members of the same family exhibit specific similarities such as Sun or Moon occupying the same signs. Gauquelin had checked the truth of these beliefs and shown that there were no zodiacal similarities among the charts of members of the same family beyond those to be expected by chance. However, the particular feature of the chart which he had already shown to be all-important where profession was concerned — planetary position in the diurnal circle — had yet to be tested.

The heredity hypothesis contains no presumption of professional success, nor does it entail any required association between planetary position and personality characteristics. All that is proposed is some observable link between the astrological indicators at the time of birth of a child and those at the time of birth of one or both parents. Thus the trial can be done with 'ordinary people'. It is not an easy trial to carry out if the times and places of birth are to be ascertained. The search for birth records across two generations for tens of thousands of cases was a gruelling task, eased only by the fact that French law requires the recording of birth time and place. In England, times are only officially recorded for the births of twins.

Gauquelin's persistence in his search for the heredity link was rewarded with success. The two important zones (just past the Ascendant and just past the culmination point) which he had discovered as potent in professional success, were again picked out in the parent/child comparisons. He found that children and one or both parents tended to share the same planets either rising or culminating. Thus if a child had Mars rising he found that one or both parents would tend to have Mars either rising or culminating. Similarly for Venus, Jupiter, Saturn and the Moon. If both parents had the same planet rising or culminating then the probability that the child would have that same planet in one of the two zones was doubled. As for the study on professionals, there were no findings above chance level for the Sun, Mercury, Uranus, Neptune or Pluto. There was no distinction between the sexes in respect of the shared planet, so that boys shared a prominent planet equally often with their mother as with their father and similarly for girls. The first study with 30,000 birth times, enabling 15,000 comparisons to be made was replicated ten years later with similar results.

These findings are of great interest for several reasons. They correspond closely with the result for professionals, both in respect of the important zones and for the reduced set of planets (Mars, Jupiter, Saturn, Moon and the one 'discovered' from the personality traits study — Venus). Furthermore, they are the only substantial results found for 'ordinary people'; some slight personality/planet effects for ordinary people have been noticed but nothing statistically significant. Finally, they open up the possibility of testing the effect of intervention with the birth process.

Intervention

Traditionally, astrologers have considered the whole of human activities to come within their purview. Thus the acts of midwives and obstetricians to hasten a birth would be only more features of life's rich tapestry steadily unrolling and there would be no reason to regard such acts as anything different from the host of separate factors influencing the original conception. If your view of astrology is that all earthly happenings — wars, earthquakes, the stock-market, elections, and horse-races — are all within the thrall of the heavenly procession, then any single human action must be subservient to the outcome. It would follow from this viewpoint that the correspondence between prominent planets at the birth times of children and of their parents would not be affected if the birth process were to be hastened by drugs. The need to test this hypothesis was, in one sense, forced on Gauquelin by the fact that in recent times the practice of inducing labour has become quite common whereas a few decades ago it was rare. Some of his birth time data were for births which had been induced and he was able to separate natural births in one collection from induced births in another. The results were quite dramatic. Where intervention had been mild, bringing forward the birth by an hour or two, the pattern of planetary occurrences was shifted so that the previously observed association would have applied at a somewhat later time. Where there was substantial intervention through surgery, the pattern disappeared and there was no apparent association between prominent planets at the child's and the parents' birth times.

This is one of the most startling findings to emerge from the Gauquelin work. Far from being 'just another of the multitude of factors', the actions of the obstetrician in bringing the birth process forward destroy the association between the planetary pattern at the child's and the parents' birth times. Any idea that the astrological dimension is so pervasive that everything becomes perfectly synchronized must therefore be discarded. The crucial experiment has been performed and we must seek alternative models for the way in which astrology works — alternative, that is, to the grand design in which everything occurs in its due season. Gauquelin is concerned that the modern practice of inducing birth (often it seems more for the convenience of the clinical staff than for the safety of the mother and child) destroys the evidence on which he has been able to work. Because the practice of induction has become so prevalent, he plans to study its effect in the case of outstanding professionals on which his first investigations were based. By taking a set of present-day outstanding athletes it should be possible to split them between natural and induced births so that any tendency for the induced birth group to lack the 'Mars effect' could be demonstrated.

Geomagnetism

Gauquelin has constantly sought explanations for his planetary correlations from orthodox science. His search among all the possibilities is set out in *The Cosmic Clocks*.[3] One of the avenues he explored led to his considering the possibility that the foetus could be responding to changes in the surrounding magnetic field. It is known that animals and human beings do have some sensitivity to magnetic fields and the earth's field does vary considerably due to solar activity. The Sun's surface is subject to tremendous bursts of activity with streams of charged particles being ejected into space and being registered on earth as magnetic storms — the source of much short-wave radio interference. Even in the relatively quiet periods between magnetic storms there are fluctuations in the earth's magnetic field which are due primarily to the Sun.

Gauquelin's test of a possible link between geomagnetic variation and the 'triggering' of births at special planetary positions consisted of separating his heredity collection of births into those occurring on days with geomagnetic disturbance and those on quiet days. He had no clear hypothesis and, if anything, expected the disturbed days to be ones in which the planetary effect would be weaker. However, the actual result was the reverse of his expectation with the correlation between prominent birth planets for parents and their children showing up twice as strongly on disturbed days as on quiet days. For him this was the beginning of a well-based physical theory to account for all of his results and indeed there were even differences among the individual planets to flesh out such a theory.

It was found that the differential between disturbed days and quiet days showed up similarly for Mars, Jupiter and Saturn but was clearly different for the Moon and Venus. In the case of the Moon, the effect hardly registered at all, while for Venus the effect was most marked of all. Such variation hints strongly at an underlying physical mechanism and recently Seymour[4] has propounded a theory based on the geomagnetic variations to be expected from planetary position. This theory is considered in more detail in Chapter 4.

The first experiment on heredity effects when the parent/child prominent planets association was discovered occurred in 1966 and Gauquelin repeated the experiment in 1976. The basic planetary associations were confirmed in the second experiment and, in addition, the geomagnetic variations were again observed. One expects that Gauquelin, with his usual meticulousness and application, would carry out a replication of any result which he reported, but this was certainly a most satisfying confirmation of a remarkable effect.

Conclusion

This completes a necessarily brief account of Gauquelin's work to date. It has been concerned with describing the main highlights and noting comparisons with traditional astrology. A survey of the modern era should record the work of other researchers, confirming the Gauquelin findings, but the replicating studies have generally been done under Gauquelin's direction even though the detailed work has been carried out by others. Other researchers have been concerned to check particular facets of his work rather than attempt new fields. For example Ertel[5] has performed a very comprehensive study on the way in which the planetary pattern fades as the group under study is drawn from less and less prominent individuals. There have been studies which carry high levels of statistical significance but lack the necessary replication exercise. For example a recent analysis of subjects having red hair[6] indicates that Mars appears in the vicinity of the Ascendant far more often than would occur by chance. To date this study has not been replicated.

3
WAVE PATTERNS

The Gauquelin Distributions

One of the striking features of the distributions of planetary position for Gauquelin's professional groups is the presence of two subsidiary maxima additional to the main peaks in the 9th and 12th houses. These smaller peaks are approximately in the 3rd and 6th houses, so that the whole pattern has the appearance of a somewhat lop-sided cross (see Figure 3). The arms of the cross are usually about 90 degrees apart but in some distributions there is substantial distortion. This kind of distortion resembles the patterns observed when two or more sets of waves are superimposed. Superimposition of waves is a common occurrence in the transmission of sound. To observe the effect the output from a microphone receiving a musical note can be fed to a cathode ray oscilloscope. For a note consisting of a pure tone with only one frequency present the trace on the oscilloscope is a sine wave as shown in Figure 4. Such a pure tone is produced by a flute, but for other instruments the pattern becomes complicated by the presence of harmonics. These harmonics are tones of higher frequency than the main note (the 'fundamental') and in fact the frequencies are multiples of that of the main note. Thus the 2nd harmonic has a frequency twice that of the fundamental, the 3rd harmonic three times that of the fundamental and so on. Figure 4 shows the oscilloscope trace for a note produced from a clarinet — the presence of a higher harmonic is clearly visible. In fact the different qualities of tone produced by different instruments playing the same note arise from the varying wealth of harmonics

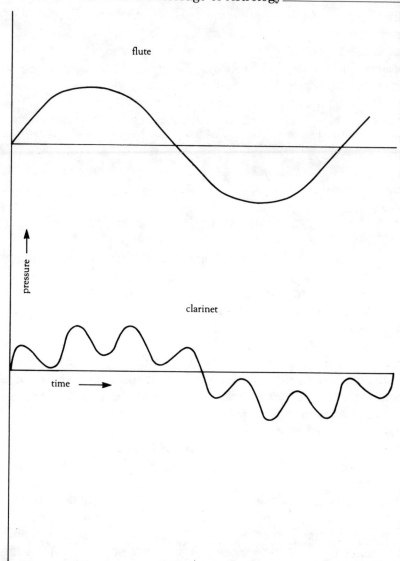

Figure 4 *Waveforms of notes produced from a flute and a clarinet.*

accompanying the fundamental.

The idea that the Gauquelin distributions consist of waves accompanied by harmonics was a natural one to occur to John Addey and myself. We had observed during study of the

distributions of Sun position in the charts of polio victims that far
from concentrating in particular signs (as one might expect from
traditional astrology) the Sun positions seemed to show wave
patterns. I had suggested to John that it would be appropriate to
use a well-known mathematical technique called Fourier analysis[1]
for deducing the harmonic content of the Sun distributions. Using
Fourier analysis we found the presence of a series of harmonics:
particularly, the 24th, 36th and 48th, each with high amplitude
and repeated for separate batches of data. This was such an
impressive result that John went on to pursue a detailed study of
harmonics in all branches of astrology and to build up a
comprehensive thesis on the subject: Harmonics in Astrology.[2] Later
in this chapter there is an account of the polio Sun distributions.

Vibrations and Waves

In order to follow the ideas involved in harmonic analysis it is
necessary to be familiar with some of the terms which are used. The
phenomenon of wave motion is pervasive and occurs in a great
variety of forms. Examples are: sound-waves in the air,
electromagnetic waves of light and radio and X-rays, seismic waves
in the earth, and ripples on the surface of water. In each case it is
possible to refer to characteristics of the wave which define it:

1. Velocity of propagation

This is the speed at which the wave travels. For example sound-
waves in air travel at about 330 metres/second.

2. Frequency

This is the number of waves emitted per second. For example the
frequency or pitch of the concert A is nominally 440 waves per
second. This is referred to as 440 Hertz.

3. Amplitude

This relates to the size of the wave. The units in which it is
measured depend on the particular wave being considered. For
example the amplitude of a wave on water (a ripple) is the
maximum height the crest of the wave reaches above the surface

of the calm water. For sound-waves in air the appropriate units are those of pressure and the amplitude is the maximum pressure above atmospheric reached in the wave.

4. Phase

Waves often arise because something is vibrating. The sound-waves from a violin are emitted because the strings are vibrating. Vibrations have frequency and amplitude, but not velocity — that is a concept confined to the waves which the vibrations may cause. In order to think of phase it is helpful to picture a slow vibration such as that of a child on a swing. Imagine two swings side by side in a childrens' playground. The two children sitting in them start together so that they both reach the lowest point together and they both reach the stationary point at the other side together. After a little while we notice that they are no longer together, or no longer 'in phase'. One child is at the lowest point when the other is at the start point — this is called 90 degrees out of phase. Still later the two children reach stationary points together but on opposite sides — this is called 180 degrees out of phase. If we wait long enough the phase difference can reach 360 degrees — this is the same as 0 degrees — they are in phase again. There is a good reason for dividing the vibration up into degrees, with a complete vibration corresponding to 360 degrees. The form of the motion is described by a sine or cosine function. Thus the position of the swing relative to its rest position is given by:

$$x = a \cos (360 \, ft)$$

Where:

x = the displacement of the swing
a = the amplitude
f = the frequency
t = the time (from zero when the swing was released)
$(360 \, ft)$ = an angle in degrees
$\cos$ = the cosine function

Figure 5 illustrates the two swings when there is a 90 degree phase difference between them and beneath the swings are the corresponding graphs of displacement with elapsed time.

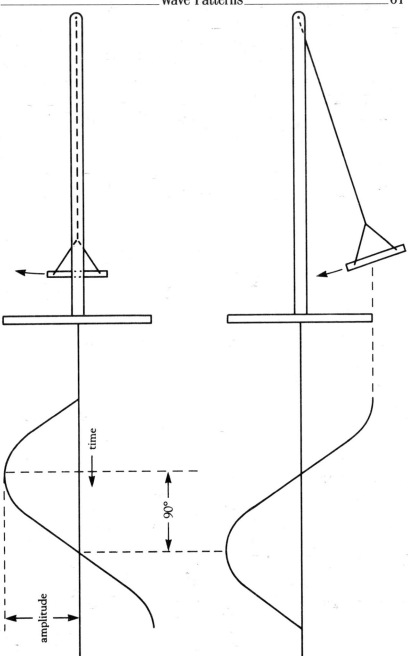

Figure 5 *Two swings 90 degrees out of phase with one another.*

5. Travelling waves and standing waves

If you hold one end of a rope which is fixed at the other end and give your end a twitch, you can observe a wave travel along the rope to the fixed end where it is reflected and returns to you. The speed with which the wave travels is determined by the tension you maintain and the 'heaviness' of the rope (how much each metre weighs). By twitching the rope in a regular rhythm you can arrange to reinforce the reflected wave and the whole rope builds up regular oscillations. These oscillations are called 'standing waves' to distinguish them from 'travelling waves', which move along the rope. In fact the standing waves arise from the presence of two waves (the forward and reflected waves) travelling in opposite directions on the same rope. A vibrating violin string exhibits standing waves. Similarly a pipe which is closed at one end can exhibit standing pressure waves if a succession of pulses travels down it to be reflected at the closed end and the timing is such as to reinforce the reflected pulses. All wind instruments make use of this effect. The frequency of the note emitted must be such that the driving and reflected pulses do indeed reinforce.

6. Harmonics

Figure 6 shows a stretched string which has been plucked and is now exhibiting standing waves with the whole string oscillating to and fro. From 5 above we know that the frequency of the oscillations must correspond to a state where a travelling wave just gets down the string and back again in the time for one oscillation. Now it is possible for a string to vibrate in a different mode. If the centre of the string is constrained and the string is plucked at either the quarter or three-quarter points then it is as if the centre point became another reflection point and the frequency doubles. The string is now vibrating in its 2nd harmonic as shown in the second diagram of Figure 6. In the same way 3rd and 4th harmonics can be generated by constraining the string at one-third or one-quarter of its length respectively. The phenomenon of harmonics is not confined to stretched strings. If you want to move up an octave when playing a recorder you 'over blow' and the little pipe emits its second harmonic which being twice the frequency corresponds to an exact octave. (Middle C is nominally 256 Hertz and the C one octave above is 512 Hertz.)

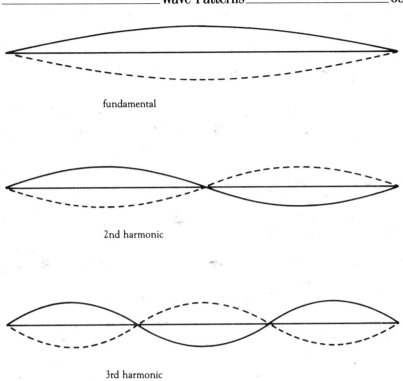

fundamental

2nd harmonic

3rd harmonic

Figure 6 *Harmonics of a stretched string.*

7. Fringes

Wave-like patterns can arise in many different ways, not just those which have been described above. One source of such patterns is a pair of grids or combs arranged parallel to one another. If the combs are viewed from a point perpendicular to the comb direction and one of them moved (while still keeping it parallel to the other) then the so-called Moire fringes are seen. Figure 7 illustrates the arrangement. Sometimes the effect can be observed when passing two parallel fences with regularly spaced uprights — some bridges with railings built over motorways provide an opportunity for drivers to see Moire fringes.

It is not at all unusual for wave patterns to be observed without its being possible to identify the causal mechanism generating the waves. For example there are a number of phenomena which

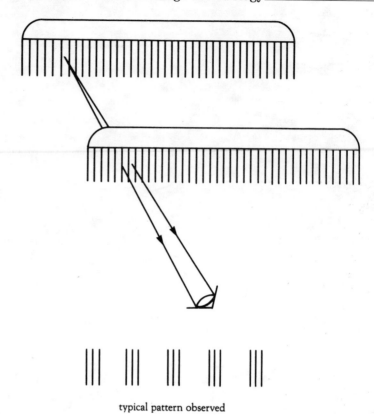

typical pattern observed

Figure 7 *Moire fringes observed with two combs.*

exhibit an eleven-year or twenty-two-year cycle and it is very likely that this is related to the sunspot cycle. The rings seen on tree stumps which portray the amount of growth occurring in each year show an eleven-year cycle quite clearly. However, the reason for the Sun undergoing periodic variation of the eruptions on its surface is not understood. The absence of complete information on the source of variation does not preclude study of the character of the variation. The early scientists who studied the wave properties of light such as interference and diffraction were not aware that the waves were actually electromagnetic in nature — that knowledge came much later.

We do not yet understand the reasons for the presence of waves in the distributions of planetary position for groups of professionals. However, the waves are just as certainly present as are the cycles in the tree rings. Furthermore the waves can be studied and their implications deduced just as the early optics researchers studied light-waves.

Harmonic Analysis

The wave patterns in the Gauquelin distributions are more like the patterns in tree rings or Moire fringes than ripples on the surface of water, because the Gauquelin distributions and the tree rings are, as it were, fossilized — they are traces of past happenings which can be examined and about which we can speculate. In contrast the ripples are dynamic; they are moving on, spreading and dying even while we look at them. Velocity of wave propagation has a meaning for ripples but not for tree rings or distributions. Three of the other terms defined previously do apply to the wave patterns in the distributions. Each wave identified has an amplitude, a harmonic number and a phase. A wave with just one crest and one trough is spoken of as the fundamental or 1st harmonic. The 2nd harmonic has two crests, the 3rd three and so on.

Figure 8 shows the wave of a 3rd harmonic, drawn in a circle rather than along a straight line as was done for previous illustrations of waves. Figure 8 also shows a 4th harmonic drawn in a circle. The amplitude of the wave in each case has been made the same.

Figure 9 shows a combination of 3rd and 4th harmonics, both with the same amplitude. The upper part of the figure shows the combined wave in a circle and the lower part as it is when set out on a straight line, with the components underneath to illustrate the arithmetic of superposition. We could go on to construct elaborate patterns by adding into the circle any number of harmonics with different amplitudes and phases. Indeed, any pattern, no matter how complicated, can be constructed by putting together enough harmonics suitably chosen for amplitude and phase.

Fourier analysis, the mathematical technique mentioned earlier, enables one to carry out the reverse process from that of constructing patterns by adding together many separate sinusoidal forms, each with its own amplitude and phase. One can take a

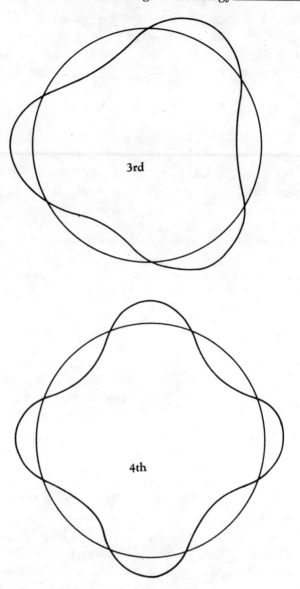

Figure 8 *Third and fourth harmonics in a circle.*

pattern and discover its harmonic content, that is to say find the amplitude and phase of each of its constituent harmonics. Figure 10 shows the distribution of Mars in the charts of prominent

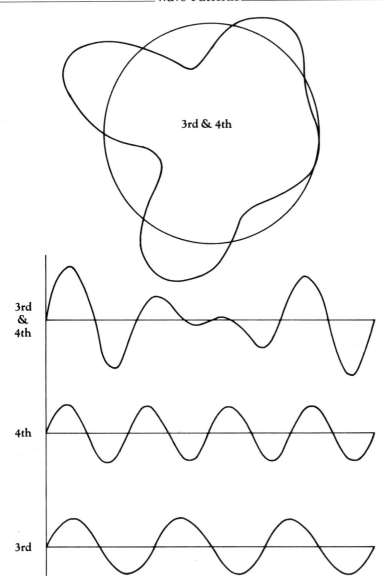

Figure 9 *Combination of third and fourth harmonics.*

athletes as found by Gauquelin. The distribution is represented by
twelve sectors. (This is the same as Figure 3 but with the sector
totals set out on a straight line instead of a circle.) Figure 10 also

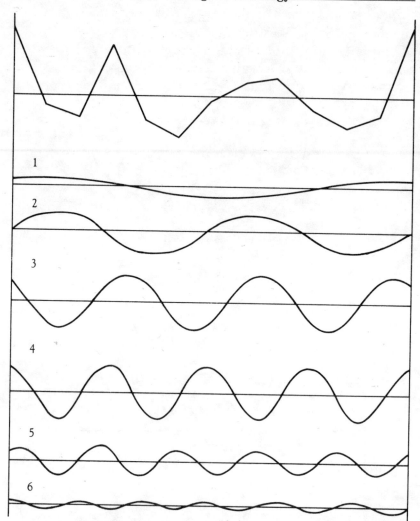

Figure 10 *Component harmonics found by Fourier analysis of the distribution of Mars in the charts of athletes.*

shows the constituent harmonics. Six harmonics are needed to describe a distribution of twelve sectors. For eighteen sectors nine harmonics are needed and for thirty-six sectors eighteen harmonics are needed. As one might expect, with more detail in the pattern, a greater wealth of harmonics is required.

It is notable that in the Mars-athletes distribution the 4th harmonic has a substantial amplitude: 12 per cent of the mean. The 4th harmonic corresponds to the 'cross' noted earlier — four crests and four troughs with the crests disposed 90 degrees apart round the circle. it was also noted that the cross was 'lop-sided'. This distortion of the cross appears because the other harmonics are present to some extent; i.e. their amplitudes are each more than zero.

Harmonics in the Gauquelin Distributions

It was noted in Chapter 2 that the distributions of planetary position in the charts of professional groups were very similar. Whether it was Saturn in the case of scientists, Jupiter in the case of politicians or the Moon in the case of writers, the patterns showed strong peaks in the regions of the 12th and 9th houses. If indeed these two peaks are just part of the 4th harmonic then it will be of interest to know how closely the 4th harmonic phase agrees among all the separate distributions. Using the 36-sector distribution,[3] harmonic analysis has been carried out on each of the profession groups. In Table 3 the number of degrees which separate the nearest 4th harmonic crest from the horizon point is

Table 3

Profession	Planet	Number of degrees between crest and horizon for 4th harmonic
military leaders	Mars	3
scientists	Mars	3.5
actors	Jupiter	1.5
athletes	Mars	9
writers	Moon	8.5
military leaders	Jupiter	1
politicians	Jupiter	9.5
scientists	Saturn	2
politicians	Moon	0.5
writers	Jupiter	4.5

shown for each planetary distribution in relation to the appropriate profession group. It is a strikingly close cluster. In order to make the clustering clearer Figure 11 shows a histogram of the in 'ividual crest position drawn on the circle.

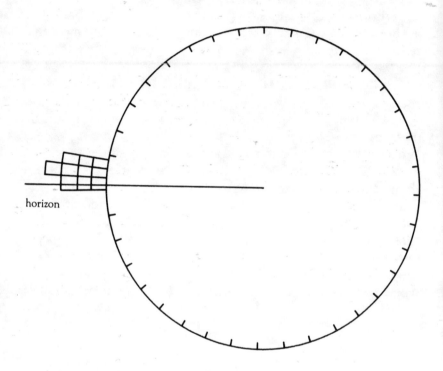

Figure 11 *Histogram of 4th harmonic peaks showing how closely they cluster.*

The approach of harmonic analysis allows of very precise comparisons between distributions. If one attempted to find the position of one of the peaks (say that in the 12th house) for each distribution then the error involved would be up to 10 degrees of the circle because a 36-sector distribution has 10 degree sectors. In order to reduce the error due to sector size, one could divide the distribution up into more sectors, say 100 or 1,000. However, this would result in each sector having only small occupancy and the pattern appearing very 'noisy'. There would be no clear peak sector. Thus there is no way to reduce the error in finding a 12th house peak unless one is able to obtain very large samples. But the Gauquelin collections are of top professionals, of whom by definition there are only relatively small numbers. In Chapter 2 it was noted that one feature of the Gauquelin research has been to show that the patterns appearing in chart collections for top professionals do not appear in collections of professionals who are in the second tier. It is apparent therefore that a barrier exists to prevent any attempt at measuring the peak position in the 9th or 12th houses.

One of the features of harmonic analysis is that the amplitude and phase of a particular harmonic derives from all of the sector totals. Thus an error in one sector total has a slight effect on either the amplitude or the phase. It is as if one were using a kind of average of the sector totals, and the average of a population is subject to much smaller error than the individual items of that population. In spite of the fact that the sectors used for the harmonic analysis are each 10 degrees long, the phases of the harmonics can still be measured to a degree of the main circle.

That the patterns appearing for separate planets and professional groups are very similar is shown by the fact that other harmonics apart from the 4th show a clustering of the phase angles. In Table 4 are listed the positions of the crests of the 3rd

Table 4

Profession	Planet	Number of degrees between crest and horizon for 3rd harmonic
military leaders	Mars	−15
scientists	Mars	−6
actors	Jupiter	−5
athletes	Mars	−7
writers	Moon	−17
military leaders	Jupiter	−13
politicians	Jupiter	−21
scientists	Saturn	−9
politicians	Moon	−8
writers	Moon	−13

harmonic for each profession group. Although not such a tight group as that for the 4th harmonic in Table 3 it is still close. This closeness of phasing among the separate distributions has one important consequence which will be explored before continuing the analysis of the harmonic array.

Velocity of the Influence

It is important to realize that the group of 4th harmonic phase positions in the histogram of Figure 11 is made up of planetary distributions in which the planets themselves are at widely differing distances from the earth. In Table 5 are shown the mean distances of the planets and of the Moon from the earth. Also listed are the times which light takes to reach the earth from each of the heavenly bodies. The values are given with a plus or minus figure for the planets because the extreme distances of a planet occur when it lies on a line joining the earth and the Sun, either on the same side as the earth or beyond the Sun and diametrically opposite the earth. As it takes light about 8 minutes to cross the distance from Sun to earth, the time of travel from planet to earth is given by the travel-time corresponding to the planet's orbital radius plus or minus 8 minutes. In the final column of Table 5 is given the approximate angle on the circle to which each time corresponds. Thus we note that for the most distant planet Saturn, its light takes some 80 minutes to reach us, so that when we observe it on the horizon, it has already moved to a point some 20 degrees above the horizon.

Table 5

Planet	Radius of orbit (millions km)	Light travel time (minutes)	Equivalent arc (degrees)
Moon	0.4	0	0
Mars	228	13 ± 8	1 to 5
Jupiter	778	43 ± 8	9 to 13
Saturn	1427	79 ± 8	18 to 22

This calculation of the time lapse involved, particularly for the more distant planets Jupiter and Saturn, points to an important consequence. If the 'appropriate' time of birth were the time when a particular planet was at the special angle above the horizon, then the phase angles would be spread out along the circle with the Moon coming first, then Mars trailing a little, Jupiter trailing still further, and Saturn bringing up the rear. The only reason that we see the phase angles clustered closely is that the important time occurs when light from the planet reaches earth. It follows that whatever 'influence' is reaching us from the planets is travelling at the velocity of light.

There is no preconception about the mechanism of planetary influence required before stating, as above, that the influence is travelling at the velocity of light. All sorts of mechanisms can be envisaged. Electromagnetic radiation given off by the planet could affect the foetus. Gravitational attraction could be the causal agent (gravitation is propagated at the same speed as light). The entire etheric 'climate' of earth at that location could be affected by the presence of the planet in the sky and foetuses along with everything else respond to it. Alternatively the foetus with its characteristics already formed could be triggered in the birth process by the planet's arriving at the 'right' place. One might envisage some form of emission from the planet which is not detectable by current instruments (rather in the same way that huge numbers of neutrinos are now known to bombard the earth continuously, but whose existence was only discovered a few decades ago). In all these cases, a connection occurs between the planet and earth; whether it be a causal link or just an information transfer makes no difference. The lower limit on the time lapse for the connection is set in exactly the same way as for any other connection in the physical universe, i.e. that given by assuming a speed of 299,800 kilometres per second. The one possibility that is ruled out is the idea of a 'grand simultaneity' of events — a planet comes to some special place and simultaneously a child is born: the two events being non-causally linked but each part of some larger design. (C. G. Jung[4] hinted at this in his theory of synchronicity.)

The Higher Harmonics

As the 3rd and 4th harmonics have been shown to be quite closely clustered, it is natural to wonder if the other harmonics exhibit similar characteristics. Figure 12 indicates the extent to which each harmonic has the phase angle from each distribution grouped. In this diagram the height of each line indicates the amplitude of the harmonic and the position of the line along the horizontal axis shows the phase angle relative to the horizon point and measured in degrees of the main circle. Thus it can be seen that the individual 4th harmonics from the set of ten distributions are grouped very tightly as has already been seen from Table 3 and the individual 3rd harmonics are less closely grouped as seen from Table 4. Of the remaining harmonics the 1st and 2nd show little clustering and are probably reflecting astronomical and demographic effects rather than anything astrological. The 5th, 6th and 7th show less clustering than the 3rd or 4th but as the harmonic number rises there is more effect from 'noise' — errors in the data — and the phase angles become more difficult to measure with accuracy. It is not valid to attempt phase angle measurement much beyond $n \div 6$ and certainly not beyond $n \div 4$ where n is the total number of sectors. (This is a mathematical point and separate from the problem of noise in the data noted above.) Hence the figure shows only harmonics up to the 7th. In spite of the spread in phase angles, it is possible to show that there is effectively a reversal (a 180 degree phase shift) if the group being studied has a contra-indicated planet.

It was noted in Chapter 2 that the distributions of planetary position fell into two groups. First were those in which the appropriate planet appeared mainly in the 9th and 12th houses. These are the 'positively indicated' cases — Mars for athletes, Saturn for scientists, Jupiter for politicians and so on. In the second group are the negatively indicated cases — the Moon for athletes, Mars for writers, etc. For this group the planet appears to avoid the 9th and 12th houses. However, this classification of being either in or out of the two houses is too crude. The harmonic pattern reveals much more detail and in Figure 13 the positively indicated amplitude and phase patterns appear above the line and the negatively indicated ones below the line. It is apparent that for

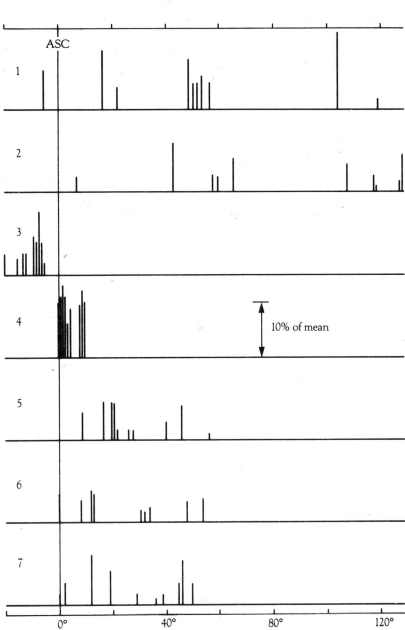

Figure 12 *Amplitudes and phases of the harmonics in the Gauquelin planetary distributions for professionals.*

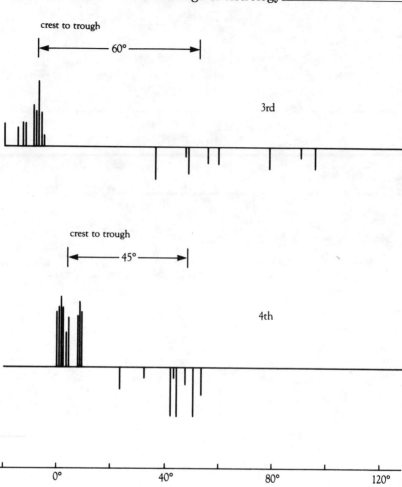

Figure 13 *Amplitudes and phases of the 3rd and 4th harmonics in Gauquelin's planetary distributions for professionals showing 'avoidance' groups below the line.*

the high amplitude and closely clustered harmonics (3rd and 4th) the two groups are oppositely phased (the crest for the first group coincides with the trough for the other). Thus the 3rd harmonic shows a separation of 60 degrees of the main circle between positively and negatively indicated groups, and similarly, the 4th a separation of 45 degrees.

Significance of the Harmonics

Given that the planetary distributions indicate the existence of harmonics which appear consistently among many disparate groups of eminent professionals and furthermore that these harmonics show distinct individual phasing, then one would expect that different meanings should apply to each of the harmonics. It was explained in Chapter 2 that in a further extension of the research on professional groups, characteristics of the members of the groups were found to be correlated with planetary position. Thus, independently of whether an outstanding individual is actually within one particular profession or another, that person's traits are found to be associated with appropriate planetary indication. Carrying the characteristics concept into the realm of harmonics, John Addey[5] carried out an experiment on the Gauquelin collection of athletes in which he split them according to sets of traits. The result is shown in Figure 14 and it can be seen that two sorts of individual defined by their respective trait lists appear in the one case as composing a 3rd harmonic and in the other as composing a 4th harmonic. In other words the harmonics correspond to particular factors which can be defined in terms of descriptive words.

If each trait set corresponds to a different harmonic then the collection of athletes contains two separate populations. Both of them have excellent athletic ability but they differ in respect of personality. Clearly, the proportion of each personality type in the whole collection corresponds to the amplitude of each harmonic. This kind of precise discrimination applied to mixed populations is possible because harmonics enjoy complete independence from one another. That is to say that one can add one harmonic after another and the resulting complex pattern shows on subsequent analysis that the phases and amplitudes of the early additions are quite unaffected by the later additions. It is as if the harmonics occupied different dimensions so that alterations of phase or amplitude in any one of them have no effect on any of the others. There is an exact analogy in the case of the radio receiver. The electromagnetic field in which the receiver is placed contains a rich collection of separate waves originating from many different transmitters, but only that frequency to which the receiver is tuned

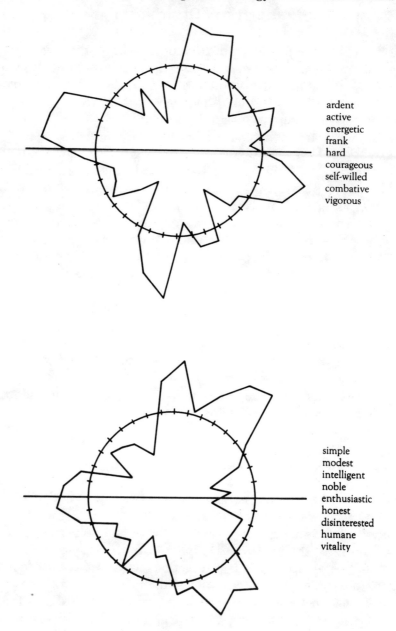

ardent
active
energetic
frank
hard
courageous
self-willed
combative
vigorous

simple
modest
intelligent
noble
enthusiastic
honest
disinterested
humane
vitality

Figure 14 *Distributions of Mars for athletes divided into two populations according to personality traits (after Addey).*

shows evidence of its presence. The receiver selects out the desired frequency by use of the phenomenon of resonance, whereas the selection of specific frequency in the Gauquelin distributions is done by Fourier analysis. However, the underlying principle enabling each of the techniques to work, is the same — that of the intrinsic independence of individual frequencies.

This idea of independence is so important to grasp, that an illustration of its working is shown in the successive diagrams of Figure 15. In the first diagram a pure 4th harmonic appears. In the second a 3rd harmonic with 50 per cent amplitude has been added. In the third diagram there is equal 3rd and 4th, while in the remainder the process is continued with the 4th diminishing to 50 per cent and finally a pure 3rd appearing at the bottom of the figure. Throughout these stages the phases of each harmonic have remained exactly the same, as found from Fourier analysis. Each behaves as if the other were not there.

The Phase Patterns

In view of the fact that there appear to be special phase angles which each harmonic adopts within the main circle, and that these same phase angles persist among the separate professional groups and throughout the set of planets which are influential, it is worth investigating these angles to see if any particular geometrical spacing is apparent. Figure 12 shows that the crests of successive harmonics are spaced further and further from the horizon point. The 3rd lies about 10 degrees below the horizon, the 4th is about 5 degrees above it and the remaining harmonics are further still above the horizon. The actual separations between successive harmonics suggest that there may be a common location for the troughs of the harmonics rather than for their crests. In order to see how this works, the trough positions for each of the sets of harmonics have been drawn in Figure 16. The method for constructing these diagrams is to add the angle between crest and trough to each of the individual harmonic phases. Thus for the 3rd harmonic group each member of the group has 60 degrees added to the crest phase angle (the angle used in Figure 12). The group is now centred at about 50 degrees above the horizon point. The added angle was 60 degrees because the 3rd harmonic has three

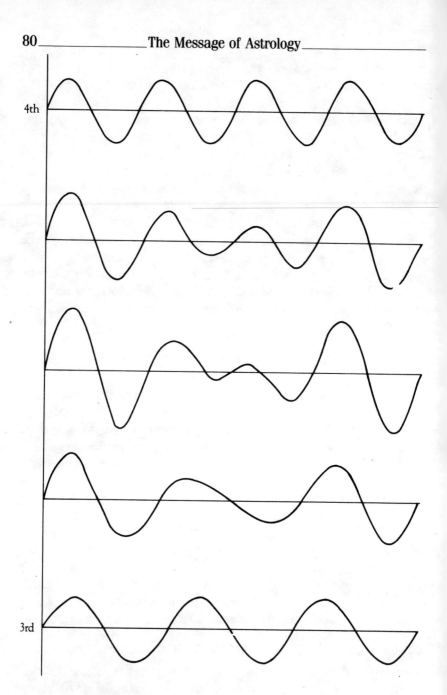

Figure 15 *Third and fourth harmonics combined with different amplitudes but keeping the same phase.*

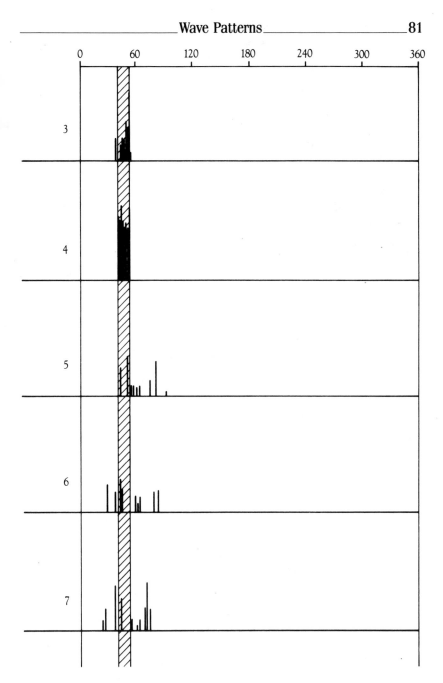

Figure 16 *Harmonics 3 to 7 in Gauquelin's planetary distributions for professionals showing positions of troughs nearest to the horizon.*

complete waves in the whole circle; therefore each wave occupies 120 degrees and the interval between a peak and the next trough is 60 degrees. In the same way each member of the 4th harmonic group has 45 degrees added to the crest phase angle because the 4th harmonic has four complete waves in the circle — each one occupying 90 degrees and the peak/crest separation is therefore 45 degrees. For each member of the 5th harmonic group 36 degrees is added, for each member of the 6th 30 degrees is added, and for each member of the 7th 26 degrees. The resulting trough groups occupy a similar region above the horizon — a vertical band has been added to indicate the region. The troughs lie at about 50 degrees above the horizon point.

In order to appreciate the overall pattern of waves it is necessary to see them all drawn in the same circle. However, if the usual illustration of sinusoidal wave forms is used the picture becomes too complicated and one cannot discern the principal symmetries. For this reason a variant of the usual means of marking wave patterns has been adopted in Figure 17. The crests of each wave have been indicated with small ellipses and each wave has been give a separate circle, so that the 3rd harmonic is in the outer circle, the 4th is on the next smaller radius circle and the 5th, 6th and 7th on successively smaller circles. This diagram has been constructed using a common trough point at 50 degrees above the horizon (which was derived from Figure 16).

It is clear that there is an intriguing symmetry about the phasing of the separate harmonics. If we stop thinking of this pattern as being a harmonics phase diagram, we can note that Figure 17 has the appearance of an open flower with its trumpet facing towards a point about 50 degrees above the horizon. The petals of the flower are disposed in a regular array about an axis of symmetry which is aligned with this point. What sort of 'sunlight' is this flower facing towards? From previous analysis of the phase clusters it was deduced that the 'influence' travels at the speed of light. For the influence to have an effect there must be a receptor organ, and this pattern suggests the form of the receptor. It is 'as if' there were a set of petal-like vanes arranged radially from a common centre. One could assume that a ray will only stimulate a petal if there is close alignment of the direction of the ray with the orientation of the petal.

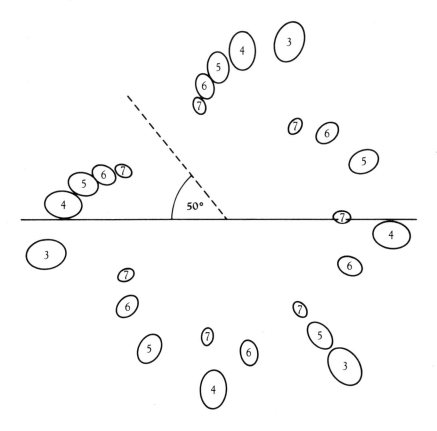

Figure 17 *Harmonics 3 to 7 in Gauquelin's planetary distributions for professionals showing positions of the peaks.*

There is a phenomenon characteristic of waves and the vibrations in pipes, strings, radio receivers, etc., to which reference has already been made — resonance. If a wave impinges on a vibrator whose natural frequency is close to that of the wave then vibrations are induced. This effect is easily appreciated by pushing a child on a swing. Provided that one pushes at the stationary point just as the down swing is starting then each push increases the amplitude. If a radio receiver is tuned to 600kHz then electromagnetic waves of that frequency will cause resonance and the signals will be received. If the influence reaching the petals of the receptor has a wave character then it is reasonable to suppose that a petal suitably aligned would resonate. This concept of resonance provides the basis of a possible mechanism which is explored more closely in the next chapter.

Other Harmonic Effects

Apart from harmonics in the Gauquelin distributions there appear to be wave patterns in other distributions. The first collection which was subjected to harmonic analysis was of victims of poliomyelitis. John Addey taught in a hospital for children suffering from this disease and it was natural for him to consider the possibility that these children would share some astrological indicator. In England there is no requirement to record times of birth except for those of twins so it is much more difficult to carry out research into patterns of diurnal positions than for subjects born in Continental countries. Michel Gauquelin extended his research across several European countries but could not attempt replication of his work in the UK because of this drawback. Thus John Addey's analysis of the polio children was conducted on the dates of birth but not the times. Even without the birth time one can study the variation of occupancy of the signs by particular planets. Many attempts have been made to discover preponderances of particular planets in signs for collections of subjects such as the polio children. Reference was made in Chapter 1 to the relative lack of success that has been achieved in such attempts. Occasionally the results rise to the level of statistical significance, but the effects are weak — a matter of only a few per cent variation from the mean.

John observed that the variation in Sun occupancy of the signs was unremarkable for the polio collection, but that the degree by degree variation round the zodiacal circle showed some striking periodicities. There are some simple ways of investigating particular named periodicities. If one suspects that say a 10th harmonic is present with substantial amplitude then the data from each of the degree occupancies — all 360 of them — can be assembled in thirty-six subtotals. The number in the first degree is added to that in the 37th, the 73rd, the 109th, etc. Then the number in the 2nd degree is added to that in the 38th, the 74th, the 110th, etc. This procedure results in thirty-six subtotals and if these are plotted as successive ordinate values along a straight line, the pattern will, apart from general clutter, show a single crest and a single trough, if indeed there is a strong 10th harmonic present. The presence of each harmonic which is a multiple of 10, i.e. the 20th, 30th, etc., up to the 180th, is also revealed, but all other harmonics are excluded by the subtotalling process.

The method described above was used to demonstrate the presence of a set of harmonics which were multiples of twelve — particularly the 24th, 36th and 48th. Confirmation that these harmonics were indeed present at substantial amplitudes was obtained from a full analysis of the original distribution. Moreover a second set of data, subsequently collected and analysed, revealed the same prominent harmonics with materially the same phase angles. Figure 18 shows the results from the two collections with the totals assembled to show harmonics which are multiples of 12. Thus the occupancy in degree 1 is added to degree 31, 61, 91 up to 331, and that of degree 2 added to degree 32, 62, etc. These thirty subtotals have been grouped in ten sets of three to show the main features of the pattern. The correlation coefficient of the two distributions is 0.77 and the probability of this arising by chance is 1 in a 100. The chi square value for the combined distributions also yields this same level of significance.

The presence of harmonics in the distribution of Sun position for collections of similar individuals is not confined to polio victims. John Addey investigated other groups and found prominent harmonics from the degree totals. An account of this work appears in *Harmonics in Astrology*.[2]

The mechanism associated with these 'solar' harmonics is seemingly different from that applying to the planetary harmonics of the Gauquelin distributions. In the first place the horizon plays no part in solar harmonics, so that a particular zodiacal degree occupied by the Sun is the same for all births anywhere on the earth's surface (or indeed some way distant from the earth). This is quite unlike the harmonics of the Gauquelin distributions, where the location of birth is as crucial as the time. It would seem that the influence deriving from the Sun, or from the combination of Sun and zodiac, is suffusing the earth — bathing it in a glow rather like sunlight except that it operates as well during the night as the day, and its character is changing every few degrees.

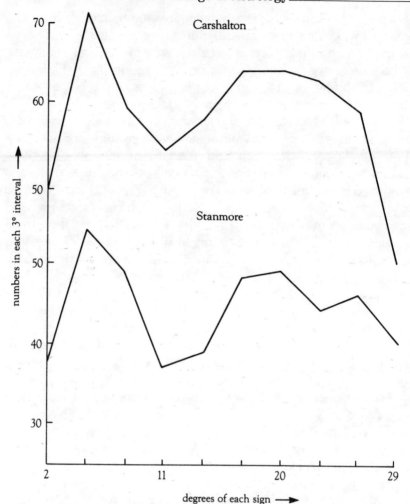

Figure 18 *Distribution of Sun in the signs for victims of poliomyelitis (two separate sets of data from different hospitals).*

It would be easier to perceive the underlying structure which gives rise to the solar harmonics if there were many similar examples of the same harmonics from different collections, as has been noted for the harmonics of the Gauquelin distributions, but so far the harmonics found in solar distributions have come in a variety of groups (e.g. multiples of 12, of 7 and of 5) and it is difficult to see any straightforward rationale for them. Possibly with more extensive investigations, the overall pattern will become as obvious as it is now for the Gauquelin distribution harmonics. After all, the Gauquelin patterns only emerged as the collections were extended over a wide range of professions.

Recapitulation

This chapter has covered a lot of material and a recapitulation is appropriate. The idea of introducing descriptions based on wave forms stems from the fact that the Gauquelin distributions look as though they have started from a wave pattern with four crests but have been distorted — presumably by the presence of other wave patterns with different numbers of crests. In order to explore this further the technique of Fourier analysis was used to uncover the wave content of each of the distributions. A general account of vibrations and waves was given so that the terms used to describe them could be readily understood. In particular the terms *frequency, amplitude, phase* and *harmonic* were illustrated. It was found that the 4th harmonic of each Gauquelin distribution is present with high amplitude and phased so that there is a crest at about 5 degrees above the horizon. The 4th harmonic phase degrees from each distribution cluster very closely together and this has one important implication — the 'influence' reaching us from the planets is travelling at just the velocity of light. If this were not so, the distribution featuring Saturn would have its crest some 20 degrees away from the crests of those distributions featuring the Moon; because light takes some 80 minutes to reach us from Saturn and during that time the earth has rotated about 20 degrees. In fact, it is the apparent position of the planets which matters, i.e. where they appear to be when the light from them reaches us.

The 3rd harmonic of the distributions also clusters quite closely and the higher harmonics to a lesser extent. The significance of the separate harmonics is brought out clearly by Addey's experiment of separating the collection of athletes into two types (what one might term the 'Olympians' and the ambitious). These correspond respectively to the 3rd harmonic and the 4th harmonic. It can be stated that the proportion of each type present in the whole collection is pro rata to the harmonic amplitude in each case.

The positioning of the harmonic crests suggests that they are parts of a more general pattern and this possibility was investigated by plotting the troughs rather than the crests. The plot showed that the troughs of the separate harmonics lined up (within the limits set by 'noise' affecting the higher harmonics). Using the trough line-up angle of 50 degrees above the horizon, a diagram was constructed of all the harmonic crests from the 3rd to the 7th using small ellipses to represent the crests rather than sinusoidal forms. This diagram has a quite striking symmetry and evokes the notion of a flower shape. It was suggested that the flower pattern could be thought of as representing a receptor organ rather than just a map of the harmonic phase positions. The 'petals' would correspond to separate receptors of the 'emanations' striking them from space. The reception process could take place through resonance if the emanations are wave-like in character and can set the petals into vibration.

The presence of harmonics in other distributions was noted, in particular the harmonics in the solar zodiacal distributions of poliomyelitis victims. There are strong harmonics whose numbers are multiples of 12 (24th, 36th and 48th) and this pattern came out clearly in a replication with polio victims from another hospital. No obvious connection exists between harmonics in solar distributions and harmonics in the diurnal circle so the solar harmonic field awaits further research.

Explanations

There has already been a hint of what kinds of process may be involved in the generation of astrological effects. When reference was made to a 'receptor organ' and to 'emanations', the outline of a possible model to explain the presence of harmonics was being sketched. These ideas will be developed later, but first a summary of the main theories that have been offered to explain astrology will be presented in the next chapter. It was necessary to have a clear picture of what has to be explained before considering the claims of rival theories.

4
THEORIES

On the whole, astrologers are not much given to theorizing. The prevalent attitude is summed up by: 'It works, so what does it matter how it works.' If one thinks of the role of professional astrologers as that of busy practitioners whose prime duty is to their clients, then this attitude is not unreasonable. Engineers do not spend much time contemplating the mystery of Newton's laws — they are quite content if the laws operate unfailingly. Doctors are more concerned with prescribing than they are about the origins of the genetic code.

Very few scientists have taken a serious interest in astrology. There are two reasons for this. First there appears to be a difference of paradigm — the universe as viewed by the scientist and by the astrologer are too different for there to be a ready meeting of minds. Secondly, there is an aura surrounding astrology suggestive of mystification, fraudulence and credulity. So strong is this whiff of chicanery that any scientist 'dabbling' in astrology risks his professional reputation.

The handful of thinkers who have attempted to come to grips with the hard core of astrological fact have been drawn from the ranks of philosophers and writers — plus one or two mainstream physicists. The theories that they have advanced can be placed in one of three categories:

1. Extensions to orthodox science

There was a time when tides were just one of the manifestations of nature like growth and decay. However, in due course it was shown that tidal motion is simply another aspect of the gravitational fields which permeate the solar system. To put it crudely one could say that the Moon caused the tides. Tidal action had been brought within the ambit of science — tides could be 'explained' by science. No new concept had to be invoked; the apparatus of science (post Newton) was adequate to answer all queries about tides.

In the same way, there are some who believe that it will be possible to explain all the phenomena of astrology in terms of orthodox science, with a few extensions of application, but with no new concepts. Gauquelin held this opinion (though some of his recent writing suggests a leaning towards symbolic interpretation[1]) and likewise Seymour,[2] who has recently put forward physical mechanisms to account for the Gauquelin distributions.

2. Metaphysics

There are those who believe that our current model of the universe is inadequate to understand the workings of astrology and that only a new vision of reality will enable us to understand how astrology fits in with everything else. In this category are Jung's ideas on synchronicity[3] and Elwell's concept of the 'cosmic loom'.[4]

3. Superscience

There have been numerous examples of the devising of new concepts within the framework of science to explain phenomena which could not be fitted into the existing set of entities and laws. Indeed one could argue that the evolution of science has proceeded by the invention (or possibly 'discovery') of new entities, fluxes and fields. Some of these inventions are found to contain flaws and are abandoned. The concept of phlogiston was discarded. At any one time textbooks contain the survivors among all those hopeful theories put forward to explain the diverse array of forms and functions that surround us. It is interesting to consider a recent newcomer on the scene — the theory of morphic resonance, advanced by Sheldrake.[5] Conscious of the inadequacies of current theories to account for the characteristic forms and behaviours of living things, Sheldrake postulates the existence of 'morphic fields' which can influence the manner in which creatures grow and learn. As so often happens, proposals for radically new models are greeted sceptically by the orthodox establishment and Sheldrake is receiving short shrift. However, if enough favourable evidence accumulates, Sheldrake's theory may become the new orthodoxy. It seems likely that models which could explain the heterogeneous collection of evidence for astrological effects will need to go beyond the boundaries of contemporary science.

Simple Beam Theories

The very fact that we can see the planets indicates that electromagnetic radiation in the form of visible light is reaching us from them. For those planets not visible to the naked eye we can use a telescope to verify that emission (or rather, reflection) of light is occurring. With the advent of radio telescopes it has been discovered that radio waves are emitted by Jupiter. In addition to reflecting and emitting electromagnetic waves the planets exert gravitational forces. With this wealth of physical 'influence' it is natural to conjecture that waves or gravitational forces could be the source of astrological effects. However, it is not difficult to show that such a simple beam theory is untenable. Astrological effects such as planetary position in the diurnal circle require that the influence persists even when the planet is below the horizon and any electromagnetic waves from the planet are blocked out by the earth. The penetration into the earth's crust of even long-wave radio waves is quite small and quite inadequate to produce any detectable effect through the crustal thicknesses involved.

Alternatively, gravitational forces have been suggested as the source of the influence. Gravitation is propagated at the speed of light and the gravitational field of a body is exerted independent of the presence of other bodies — which overcomes the difficulty of the intervening earth opaque to electromagnetic waves. This time the problem is the extreme smallness of the force to be detected compared with the earth's background gravitational field. It is quite beyond the capacity of our instruments to register on earth the separate gravitational force due to, say, Mars. Indeed it has been estimated that the gynaecologist exerts more gravitational force on the foetus than Mars! There is really no prospect of any simple beam theory explaining the evidence.

Midwife Planets

Whereas simple direct beam theories are inadequate there is always the possibility of indirect influence. Gauquelin[6] had a strong predilection for a theory firmly based within the range of contemporary scientific knowledge. It was noted in Chapter 2 that one of his findings concerned the variation of correlation between parent and child prominent planets with geomagnetic disturbance. On geomagnetically disturbed days there was twice the frequency of parent/child agreement of prominent planets as on quiet days. The idea that human beings are sensitive to small changes in the local magnetic field is not unreasonable. Gauquelin looked into the work of Rocard,[7] who carried out investigations on dowsing — attempts to detect the presence of underground water. Rocard discovered very weak changes in terrestrial magnetism caused by the presence of water in the soil, which could produce a relaxation in the dowser's muscles — and a twitch of his hazel twig. In the course of his trials, Rocard found that the capacity for detecting weak magnetic gradients is not particularly rare or confined to professional dowsers. In addition to explaining the dowsing effect this work also revealed the source of some anomalous dowsing experiences: such as the reaction to buried metal objects which produce magnetic gradients similar to those found accompanying underground water.

The ability to detect weak magnetic gradients is only part of the whole picture and other researches were investigated to meet the gaps that still exist in a physical theory which could account for birth time and planet correlations. Gauquelin delved into a variety of experimental work, particularly that of Brown[8] who had discovered that some animals have accurate biological clocks. Brown showed that even in complete darkness and removed from all sensory clues such as temperature change, some animals could maintain their body clocks with great precision. In addition to maintaining the internal clock's regularity he demonstrated that oysters react to cosmic influences and can adjust their rhythms to changes in the cosmic background. He had some live oysters sent in closed, darkened containers from Long Island Sound to his laboratory in Evanstown, a thousand miles from the sea. On arrival their activity was observed by measuring the opening of their valves and it was found that over some days their daily rhythm adjusted so that they opened up at the time the tide would have flooded Evanstown, had the town been by the sea, i.e. when the Moon passed over the local meridian. The oysters were no longer reacting to actual tides but were responding to the lunar cycle (while still in the dark tanks they had occupied since their transportation).

Brown's oyster experiments were not the only ones that showed a sensitivity of animals to the cosmos without there being any direct sensory knowledge of Sun or Moon. Thus Gauquelin had a further potential linkage to include in a physical theory and he could sketch the main lines of it. The child in the maternal womb is well shielded from environmental clues. Like Brown's oysters the child is maintained in darkness at a constant temperature and these conditions would seem ideal for sensitivity to the cosmic stimuli. It is known that an extremely small amount of hormone in the blood is sufficient to produce childbirth and it can be supposed that a cosmic stimulus may induce such a minute hormonal secretion. The actual transmission of the stimulus may be via magnetic field changes and this would tie up with the findings on geomagnetism. Gauquelin called his theory 'The Midwife Planets' because the central core of the theory was the planetary trigger at time of birth — a planet ushering in the birth and so playing the role of cosmic midwife.

One of the obvious advantages of such a theory is that there is no need to invoke any actual physical influence on the personalities of individuals as they are being born. The theory proposes simply that certain sorts of people tend to get born at specific times. As the birth time approaches, if the child has martian qualities then it will be Mars that triggers the birth and if saturnine qualities then Saturn will do the triggering. The theory has the further virtue that it can explain the intervention effects. If the birth is brought forward by the obstetrician then this will override the trigger and a shift in the planetary patterns will result (or a loss of pattern if the intervention is drastic).

Gauquelin was aware of a problem in his theory and with his usual honesty exposed it to view. The correlation of planetary position with birth time requires the timing to be accurate to within at most an hour or so. The actual accuracy is probably better than that if one considers the phasing of the harmonics described in Chapter 3. However, the onset of labour in most cases takes place well before birth which means that a first trigger for the initiation of labour is required to operate some time before the final trigger that signals the birth itself. The first trigger presumably requires some cosmic stimulus so where are the planets at the onset of labour? Gauquelin spent some effort in attempts to discover anything significant about planetary position at the onset of labour (as opposed to the birth time) but the results were not conclusive. Because of this intractable problem of the interval between start of labour and birth (and possibly for other reasons) Gauquelin appears currently to be less inclined to favour a physical model which could explain his results and in his most recent book[1] has seemed to incline towards symbolism as the answer.

A New Magnetic Theory

Gauquelin was assembling his theory in the late 1960s and using results of researches up to that time. There has been quite a lot of new knowledge acquired since then and the scope for a more convincing physical theory has expanded. Recently Seymour[2] has proposed a theory which draws on this new knowledge. He is an astronomer who has specialized in space magnetism and was attracted to the possibility of an explanation for the Gauquelin findings when he realized the significance of the heredity correlations changing with geomagnetic activity. If indeed the astrological influence was ultimately a magnetic one then it was right in his specialist area.

In order to understand Seymour's theory it is necessary to appreciate that the space around the Sun and stretching away towards the planets is far from empty. There are colossal storms occurring on the Sun and streams of charged particles are thrown off. This wind of particles can impinge on the earth's atmosphere and create the aurora borealis or northern lights. The reason that the lights are seen in higher latitudes is that the particles follow curved paths in the earth's magnetic field. The solar wind has its own magnetic field and its effect is to distort the magnetosphere of the earth. Now the storms on the Sun are influenced by the planets. This is a gravitational effect and larger influences occur when planets are in positions that reinforce (conjunctions and oppositions). Thus we have a gravitational connection between the planets and the Sun, plus a connection between Sun and earth via the solar wind. Hence there is a connection between the planets and earth. This is the link that Gauquelin could never substantiate. He could only infer the planetary influence from evidence on lunar and solar influences.

The mechanics of the planetary influence which Seymour proposes is complex. It has been noted already that the planets' gravitational fields are weak at the earth (and at the Sun) so it would be surprising if substantial effects could be traced to these unaided fields. However, Seymour observes that the phenomenon of tidal resonance can produce great amplification. For example the tidal rise and fall of the sea which we can observe is, in most locations, quite small (in mid ocean it is negligible). Where there is the possibility of resonance then great amplification can occur. What is needed is a basin with a natural period of filling and emptying close to that of the Moon's passage between two opposed points (there are two tides a day at most places). Such a basin exists in Canada — the Bay of Fundy — and this bay experiences rise and fall of some tens of feet. The behaviour of the magnetic lines of force which spread out from the Sun has something in common with that of fluid behaviour and one can speak of 'solar magnetic canals'. There can be resonant amplification of the weak tidal forces of the planets on the Sun by the solar magnetic canals.

Given that the magnetic field of the earth is varying and these variations find their source in the Sun's activity which in turn is influenced by the planets, we have the basis for a causal influence. Seymour envisages the changing magnetic fields being responsible for electric currents which can cause impulses to pass along the nerve cells of the nervous system. These impulses can then leave their imprint on the brain of the foetus in the form of rudimentary memories. This provides the final link from planets to people and Seymour goes on to work out the further consequences which would follow.

Any theory should be able to explain important details of the phenomena to which it applies. Perhaps the greatest triumph of Seymour's theory is to demonstrate that the tidal variations applying to the planets and to the Moon are ordered in exactly the way that Gauquelin found for his planetary variations on the geomagnetic effect. Thus for the Moon the tidal pull changes by a factor of only 50 per cent between its extreme values. For Venus the variation of tidal pull between its extremes is 200 to 1. The ratio for Mars is 100 to 1, for Jupiter 3 to 1 and for Saturn 2 to 1. Seymour points out that the tidal variation of the Moon does not require the added amplification of a magnetically disturbed day, whereas for Venus it is probably essential when Venus is furthest from the earth. Gauquelin found that his variation of heredity effect with geomagnetic disturbance was greatest for Venus, less so for Mars, smaller for Jupiter and Saturn, but negligible for the Moon. This agreement is most impressive.

Seymour is still developing his theory and we must wait to see if there are to be more correspondences such as the one described above. However, it does seem, even at this stage, that there is good reason to believe that the Seymour theory contains elements of the truth. Whether it will ultimately explain all of the evidence seems unlikely, but Seymour has said that even if there are paranormal links involved in astrology, his mission is to establish how much of it can be explained on straightforward scientific principles.

Synchronicity

Because of the difficulties in constructing a scientific theory of astrology there are attractions in seeking an explanation through metaphysics. Jung[3] proposed that astrology could consist of acausal connections. Instead of there being any influence exerted by the heavenly bodies there could be a simple collocation in time of separate events. As Mars looms over the horizon so there is the birth of a child who will later become an outstanding athlete. No causal link need exist between these two occurrences — it is just that they are synchronous. Either one can argue that there are lots of in-built clocks or it is necessary in a theory of synchronicity to postulate that the quality of time itself is changing from instant to instant. In the latter case, it is then appropriate to assert that Mars appearing and the potential athlete being born are two events that are apt for that moment in time. It is one of those wide, breathtaking statements to say that time itself has its own special quality at each instant. However, it is a great problem for any universal theory which applies to absolutely everything that it may actually be meaningless because it cannot be tested. Before coming to the difficulty of testing, there is another problem about acausality from in-built clocks to be considered.

There are lots of examples of synchronicity in the sense of collocation in time of events which are not causally related. If you think of two clocks in a room, one showing the time on its face and the other having its face covered but chiming the hours, then an observer ignorant of clocks would notice repeated coincidences. He would see that whenever the first clock showed the hour, the second clock chimed, and he might well infer that there was a connecting mechanism between them. The idea of celestial clocks is an attractive one because the solar system appears to mark the passage of time with great precision. The Sun rises day after day and the seasons succeed one another with relentless regularity. One could suppose that everything was in time with this great clock and discovering synchronicities was just like observing the two clocks in the room. However, the two clocks in the room do need winding and setting, so we must assume that all the phenomena that are going to synchronize have been 'wound and set'. This would be satisfactory if the clocks then ran to time, but we know this is not true for the earth. The day was much shorter than twenty-four hours in the distant past and in the far future it will have lengthened even more because of the friction effect of the tides. The solar system clock is not absolute — it is running down. One could imagine a celestial timekeeper who makes adjustments so that everything keeps synchronized, but if you think of the terrestrial winder and setter who looks after the two clocks in the room you realize just how significant is his role. He adjusts the two clock movements so that their speeds are very close together and then he returns at intervals to make any small adjustments so that the two clocks agree precisely. In these activities he has become indistinguishable from a spindle that connects the two clock movements together — he has become the causal connection. It is so for any celestial timekeeper: there can be no difference between such timekeeping and causality.

Even if we could accept the celestial timekeeper there is the difficulty of testing synchronicity. If two events considered to be of similar quality do actually coincide in time then we say: 'Ah, synchronicity!' but if this only happens occasionally then we say: 'There is a tendency towards synchronicity,' and if there is no more than a random clustering of similar quality events then we say: 'Clearly, we are mistaken in thinking of these events as being genuinely similar in quality.' It is impossible to devise an experiment which would distinguish between synchronicity and an alternative theory, because whatever happens can always be interpreted as being within the framework of synchronicity. There are no predictions which can be made from synchronicity which, if found to be true, would distinguish it from an alternative theory.

Let us suppose that, in some unexplained way, the objection above could be overcome. Then the 'quality of time' concept must either be local or it must affect the entire universe. It has been estimated that just within our own galaxy there are probably tens of thousands of planetary systems and within each one of these there is the possibility that one or more of the circling planets could sustain life. Are we to believe that the quality of time on one such planet is ruled by what Mars, Saturn and Jupiter are doing in our little solar system (or one should say, '. . . synchronous with Mars, Jupiter or Saturn')? When it is put in those terms, the idea sounds absurd and the alternative of a local quality of time must be preferred. Local time quality implies that we have our time quality in the solar system and inhabitants of other planets in other systems each have their own local time qualities — which are not the same as ours. Now such a proposal is well short of the grand metaphysical construction from which we started. If time quality is local then just how local can it be? It could, for example, be like temperature which is a local quality. As one moves over the surface of the earth so one experiences the local temperature wherever one happens to be. All sorts of phenomena are affected by the local temperature. The freezing of water, the germination of seeds, the fermentation of wine . . . However, there is no need to invoke any mysterious local quality to explain the way temperature works. It is just another causal factor. If the temperature drops below 0°C water freezes and if the temperatures rises again it thaws. If time itself has a local quality then its effects are going to be indistinguishable from ordinary causal factors, and it can be investigated just as we investigate ordinary causal factors.

The kinds of difficulty noted above concerning testing and the universal/local problem afflict particularly those theories which involve a grand metaphysical new vision of reality, though there are lesser constructions which run the same risk. Popper[9] has criticized Darwinian evolution as not being a proper theory — in the scientific sense of being strictly testable. Is it possible to construct an alternative to evolution and then to construct a test experiment which would distinguish between them? The answer is probably 'no'; but evolution can be defended on the grounds that it is the only explanation which is consonant with the body of scientific knowledge, i.e. which does not invoke arbitrary interference by a deity. The fact that even theories within the main corpus of science run the risk of being vacuous, i.e. of being strictly untestable, indicates how much care is necessary in constructing theories about astrology which avoid this same trap.

The Cosmic Loom

A metaphysical explanation for astrology has been advanced by Denis Elwell. He is an astrologer using essentially orthodox astrology, and who has little time for the Gauquelin work, regarding it as of only slight import. He has set out his theory, accompanied by much supporting material, in *Cosmic Loom: The New Science of Astrology*.[4] Elwell's thesis is that reality is more complex than we ordinarily perceive it to be. In everyday life we have a window on reality in only one direction, whereas there are hidden dimensions. In a graphic illustration he uses the example of an orange. If you cut the orange in half, you may see either two semicircular shapes separated by a diametral line, or a ring of sectors — depending on the orientation of the cut. He suggests that reality is similar to the orange. Our conventional view finds one set of categories: the sort that are listed in Roget's *Thesaurus*; but there exists another set of categories which are just as much part of the same reality. Astrology has always contained collections of apparently very disparate items under the governorship of a single planet or a single sign or a single house. Elwell points out that modern science is rediscovering some of these collections. It is only lately that bones and gravity (both under Saturn) have been discovered to have a strong link, as space medicine reveals that weightlessness causes the bones to dissolve. Another modern finding is that lead, also included in

Saturn's category, has an affinity with the bones and tends to be stored there. This exploration of Saturn's 'warp' strand in the cosmic loom is carried forward to connect with further examples of structure, ageing, cooling and gloom — all Saturnian matters. A very persuasive case is made for a set of categories which coexist with our conventional ones. By ordinary standards the mix of items in these categories is bizarre. As an example consider the list of matters and occupations as appropriate to the sign Capricorn according to Hone in *The Modern Textbook of Astrology*[10]:

Cold	Civil servant
Concentration	Mathematician
Crystallography	Osteopath
Discontent	Politician
Gates and doors	
Old age	
Orderliness	
Responsibility	

Elwell advocates that research be pursued into demonstrating and extending these sets of categories. He sees a whole science waiting to be explored. It is an intriguing vision of another landscape that he offers and it deserves careful scrutiny to understand how its reality could be established. Some points relevant to this task of proving the cosmic loom are listed below:

1. If the categories are real then they must be shown to arise more than would be generated by chance coincidences. The difficulty is that if you are seeking for groupings then you find them whether or not they are 'really there'. It seems that we are predisposed to 'see' groupings in random arrays. This is easy to demonstrate using arrays which have been generated randomly and asking people to say whether they think the results are actually random. Invariably, the answer (at least from non-statisticians) is that the array contains clusters. Figure 19 shows events generated by a Poisson process, i.e. one in which the probability of an event occurring within each equal interval of time is the same. To most people this array appears to contain clusters and they doubt that it is 'really random'. However, there are statistical tests

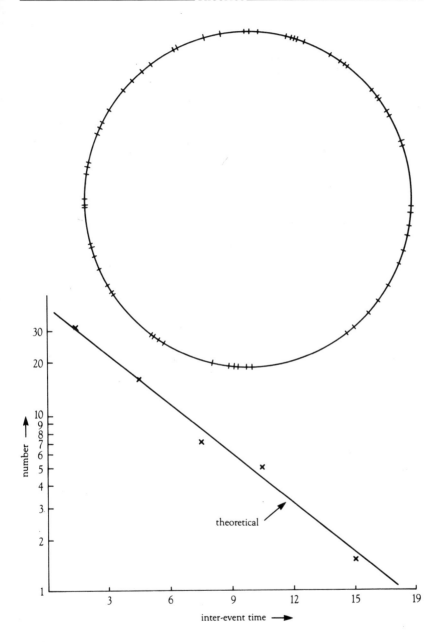

Figure 19 *Typical stream of events for a Poisson process (upper) and plot of the inter-event times (lower).*

to check whether there is any significant departure from randomness. For a genuinely Poisson process, the inter-event times should be distributed according to a negative exponential function. Figure 19 also shows a plot of inter-event times for the array and it is apparent that there is approximate conformation with the theoretical for comparison. In fact, agreement between the plot and the expected line is such that closeness of this order could be expected more often than not; i.e. there is no reason on statistical grounds to assert that this array has non-random clusters present.

The same kind of pitfall is present if one is looking at apparent clusters of planet or sign or house indicators. Elwell offers several examples of the clustering indicators. In one of these he points out that a man's interest in music could suggest either Venus or Neptune, but if he also had sailing as a hobby then Neptune would be the obvious choice. In fact, former prime minister Edward Heath has these two recreations and indeed has Neptune in the 5th house (recreations come under 5th house matters). In demonstration of further items in the cluster, Elwell notes that Edward Heath's yacht was called *Morning Cloud* and Neptune has its root in a word that means 'cloud' and which also supplies nebula and nebulous. How are we to judge whether this little collection of items is statistically significant — or rather whether lots of such collections are, as a whole, significant? For it is being suggested that though one such grouping could be coincidence, a host of them raises the level of significance way beyond chance. The difficulty here is that once someone is convinced then they find confirmation everywhere — indeed they have become conditioned to find such confirmatory indicators: they can filter them out of the mass of data which bombard us in everyday life. It is as if you were told that a room was characterized by lots of things in it having C as their initial letter: ceiling, carpet, curtains, chairs, candles . . . Well perhaps, until you note that if S had been chosen you could have listed: sofa, shelves, switch, stool, socket . . . There really must be a test comparable with that used for checking the apparent clustering in a string of events generated by a Poisson process. However, statistical technique is not well suited to tests on collections of the sort that astrology predicts. To take the case of the items in the room and the question of whether C dominates their initial letters, one would have to list all the room items and count all those beginning with A, with B, etc., through to Z in order to decide the answer. A comparable check for a collection of disparate items drawn not just from a room but from all existence is daunting indeed, especially when it is realized that this must be done repeatedly on separate collections in order to build up to a convincing level of significance. The advent of the computer has brought this sort of task within the bounds of possibility, but one would want some indication of the prospect of success before embarking on it. Simpler and more restricted tests can be pursued more readily. 'Does Neptune in the 5th house predispose to music or sailing?' is the kind of question which can be tackled in reasonable time, but here we are back with just those kinds of question which so many statistical forays into the astrological field have attempted — and with extremely limited success. It was not until the Gauquelin work that statistical evidence began to look really interesting. Now Gauquelin could find no evidence of any cc relation between Neptune house position and profession. This bodes poorly for any more elaborate exercise on the astrological categories.

The reality of the astrological categories must remain an open question. It may be that more ingenious tests could be devised to probe it, but until that comes about, we cannot be sure.

2. Given that the cosmic loom may still be a good description of reality, what does it say about the diverse array of evidence thrown up by the Gauquelin work and its ramifications through the harmonics? Well it is difficult to discern any testable consequences arising from the loom theory. The theory is not specific enough — its only novelty is the concept of an alternative view. Now that view may be very

grand in scope and positively inspiring in power, but unless it affords some means of distinguishing its truth from alternative views then it is ultimately sterile. Elwell's own opinion about testing to demonstrate the truth of astrology turns on its power of prediction. In order to further serious interest in the subject, he himself has gone out on a limb, making fairly specific forecasts of important events. A particularly impressive example of prediction was deliberately timed to precede the publication of his book. He announced that there was risk of a major shipwreck in the near future and he sent the warning to the head offices of the shipping lines. The Zeebrugge ferry disaster occurred close to the time of prediction. Though this forecast is impressive it has to be noted that it is more of a confirmation of the working of traditional astrology than a demonstration that the cosmic loom hypothesis is sound.

Requirements for a Theory

The theories discussed so far have all got serious shortcomings. The grand metaphysical designs are ultimately untestable. The theories that depend on a trigger effect to cause birth at the 'right time' founder on the need for labour to have started some time before birth occurs. Finally, the search for suitable electromagnetic waves or gravitational forces to work directly is a vain one both because of the weakness of planetary emissions or fields and the fact that the earth is opaque. The question arises of whether a theory can be constructed which would satisfy the main body of evidence which now exists. The evidence varies in quality and one would want a good theory to explain adequately all of the well-established and indisputable evidence, but perhaps only to offer possible extensions in meeting those parts of the evidence which are less secure. In order to define the requirement more closely the evidence can be divided into four tiers with the most secure in the first tier and the least well-attested in the fourth.

In the first tier is the Gauquelin work on the professional groups. It should be possible to explain why the distributions of planets at the birth times of groups of professionals follow a similar pattern and why this pattern has quite distinct features. Equally important is the task of accounting for the fact that these patterns fade away as lesser mortals are included in the groups. In addition one would want to be able to understand why there are specific heredity patterns — the same prominent planets at the birth of children and their parents. The additional fact that intervening to hasten the birth process first shifts the pattern and then destroys it should fit the theory. Finally, there is the evidence concerning geomagnetic activity. It was found that the heredity correlations were higher on disturbed days than on quiet days. Apart from the positive findings that have been summarized above, it would be reassuring if the theory could explain a number of negative findings which Gauquelin obtained. The most striking of these was the lack of any observable effects from the Sun, Mercury, Uranus, Neptune and Pluto, working in the same way as the other planets and the Moon in the charts of professionals. Although the geomagnetic findings suggest a physical basis, Gauquelin could find no evidence of varying strength of the 'influence' with varying distance of the planets from earth. When one appreciates that the distance of Mars to earth changes by a factor of 6 as the position of Mars changes from being on the same side of the Sun as earth to being on the opposite side, this finding is surprising. All the physical transmissions such as electromagnetic waves and gravitation fall off with the square of the distance.

In addition to this foundation evidence furnished by the Gauquelin research there are findings which reach a lower level of statistical significance from those described above. This lower significance occurs either because the sample size was smaller or the effect weaker (or both). There is a further qualitative point. For high confidence in the validity of a piece of statistical analysis it is necessary to replicate the work and corroborate the first conclusions. The Gauquelin work achieves this requirement whereas the 'second tier' often fails in this respect. For example the Dieschbourg results on planetary aspects which were described in Chapter 1 have not been replicated. Nevertheless, there were departures from chance levels which appear impressive and these results belong in the second tier. The solar distributions in the charts of poliomyelitis victims replicated successfully and reached significance — though not outstandingly so. There is a certain isolation about these findings in that the particular pattern of harmonics does not occur elsewhere; hence the demotion to second tier. Smithers' investigations of occupation and Sun sign used very large samples so that even tiny deviations from chance yielded statistical significance. However, the effects found were small and the work belongs no higher than the second tier.

In the third tier of research there are some reports which, if they could be verified, would be of great importance in the construction of a satisfactory theory. They concern the possible working of astrology in the mineral and vegetable kingdoms. In the 1920s Kolisko[11] performed experiments which were intended to reveal the effects of planetary influences on metal salts in solution. Typical experiments involved the precipitation of metal from solution on filter paper carried out at various times, some of which coincided with particular planetary configurations. For example, silver precipitated by ferrous iron was reported to be affected by Moon/Mars events (usually conjunctions or oppositions). The effects consisted of changes in the forms which appeared on the filter paper — there were said to be qualitative differences in the forms if planetary influence were operating. However, as subsequent workers have discovered, the experiments are very susceptible to factors such as mixing technique, the presence of organic matter, paper quality, temperature and concentration. Furthermore, the forms which appear on the paper have to be interpreted and this opens up yet another possibility for ambiguity. Replications of the Kolisko work have been attempted with varying degrees of success. Some researchers claim to have confirmed the original findings and others maintain that the variations could all be accounted for by extraneous factors.

The attraction of the Kolisko work lies in the correlation, not only of planetary events with phenomena in metal solutions, but also of metals which are themselves especially appropriate. Traditionally, the planets, Sun and Moon govern particular metals:

Sun	gold
Moon	silver
Mercury	mercury
Venus	copper
Mars	iron
Jupiter	tin
Saturn	lead

Thus it was Moon/Mars events for silver precipitated by ferrous iron. Clearly the establishment of such relationships would be important. However, at the present time, the state of the research is such that although further effort would be justified one could not yet draw any firm conclusions.

There is a fourth tier of evidence which consists of 'surprising coincidences' of the type described in the section on Elwell's theory of the cosmic loom. If there were vast numbers of such coincidences then they would cease to be surprising and we would all take it for granted that astrological influences were pervasive. Nor in that case would we need statistics to be convinced. However, it is precisely because these curious collocations in time of events are occasional and in one sense unreliable that statistical methods are essential to avoid attaching meaning to random clusters. Anecdotal evidence is not entirely useless — after all, the evidence for the existence of meteorites was at one time only anecdotal. Anecdotal material proffers hints about the form that theory should take. History suggests that before the firm establishment of phenomena there is a period with only a minority of believers prepared to vouch for the reality of the effects. It is helpful to take note of the fringe effects even though they carry much less weight than the established facts. The majority of astrologers would assert that prognostication using 'transits' is sound. A transit occurs when a planet, in the course of its motion round the Sun, crosses a point in the zodiac corresponding to a 'sensitive point' in the natal chart. When this happens it is supposed to augur happenings appropriate to the planet making the transit and to the sensitive point. There has been no published evidence yet which confirms this belief, but it could be helpful to consider whether a given theory, on trial, could supply an explanation for transit effects. The same argument applies to 'time twins' — pairs of people who are born within a very short time interval of one another and within a short distance. Although there have been some striking instances of time twins[12] who resemble one another very closely there are undoubtedly many pairs of time twins who are not particularly alike. If a theory purporting to explain the main findings of astrological research could also shed some light on the elusive evidence for time twin resemblance, that would be persuasive. There is a wider field of astrology applying to many classes of human activity. The idea behind it is that the analogy of conception and birth holds for all sorts of beginnings. For example, in the case of a ship, the birth would be the launch and the previous period of construction would correspond to gestation, with conception tying in to the first plank laid or design completion. The 'birth' of a nation state could be the signing of its constitution. The 'birth' of a marriage partnership could be the wedding. It is not difficult to discover appropriate ceremonies that could be loosely compared with the birth of a structure, an enterprise or an association. Once again, the evidence for such beliefs is anecdotal, but it would be interesting to know whether a theory could accommodate such possibilities.

In the next chapter a theory is advanced which can provide explanations for many of the research findings that have been summarized here. In addition there are indications of how the theory would be able to explain some of the more peripheral effects in astrology.

5
A NEW VITALISM

The history of science is replete with instances in which it proved necessary to devise a new model to explain phenomena which refused to be fitted into the old models. Perhaps the most dramatic example is that of the quantum theory, where energy came to be modelled as discrete lumps (though of varying size, unlike electrons or protons). Given enough hard evidence scientists have been prepared to countenance the most bizarre constructs lying behind the surface of reality. Precedent suggests that a bold approach is favoured when the evidence is flatly contrary to common sense. Michelson and Morley discovered that the velocity of light is the same measured in different directions — quite unlike the velocity of sound measured by an observer travelling through the air. For a wave travelling in a medium the movement of either source or observer results in a change of velocity. However, for light no change occurs. Up to the time of the Michelson-Morley experiment it had been common sense to conceive of light as travelling through a medium — the ether, and therefore it was clear that the velocity of the earth through the ether could be measured. The experiment not only destroyed the notion of the ether, it provided one of the fundamental facts on which the theory of relativity was based. The construction of this theory was a truly bold enterprise. Since its acceptance, commonsense reality has come to seem a very thin façade concealing things stranger than fiction.

The Gauquelin findings contradict common sense. *Ergo* something uncommon is needed to understand them. Gauquelin's own suggestion of how children come to be born at times when specific planets are in particular positions turned on the idea of a planetary trigger to stimulate birth. The difficulty, which he himself recognized, is that the birthing process is commenced some times before the actual birth.

Given an interval between the initiation of labour and parturition, the means of achieving a coincidence between birth time and planetary position involves planning. If we consider the information required for this planning to be effective, it is quite demanding. Knowledge is needed of where the particular planet will be in x hours time — in spite of the fact that it is often below the horizon and out of sight at the time that labour commences.

Planning Requirements

To refer to a 'planning' operation immediately conjures up a planner and also the possibility of the plans going awry. Indeed if plans never went awry then one could suspect the presence of immutable law. Apparently there are some tribes that drive away the 'demon' obscuring the Sun during an eclipse by beating drums. This technique always works. The Sun always reappears. The plan to release the Sun is always successful. But if it really were a plan then it could fail. If the drummer mislaid his drum or the whole tribe were engaged on more urgent business so that the demon was not driven away, then the Sun would stay hidden. Not so: the Sun always survives. The test of 'interference' is a crucial one.

The Gauquelin heredity effect is susceptible to interference. If the birth is brought forward artificially by drugs or by surgery, then the planetary patterns are either shifted in time or, if the interference is radical, the patterns fade altogether. If astrology were a universal interpenetrating influence that brought about all the planetary coincidences and arranged for everything to happen at its appointed time and place, then the obstetrician who induced labour would be just another part of that grand design and the correlations would persist as strongly as when no such interference occurs.

Given the presence of a 'planner' with very good forward knowledge of the planets and the ability to influence the birth process, but not to affect the actions of those exterior to the mother, whereabouts should we look? The entity sought is not some far-seeing providence because such a being could certainly take account of the occasional interfering obstetrician. On the other hand, the requisite powers are inappropriate to anything we know about the unborn foetus. Arguably, the foetus possesses powers that are not manifest except in the special circumstances immediately prior to birth, but this seems unlikely because there is no supporting evidence of special powers.

The concept of planning and choosing suggests that some advantage derives from choosing correctly; i.e. it is in some sense worthwhile to be born at the 'right time'. The advantage of being born at the right time is clearly not overwhelming. There is no obvious difference between children who are born naturally and those whose births were artificially induced. There exist so many people in this latter category during the present era that even small differences would have been noticed by now. In fact Gauquelin's argument that the characteristics of the child already exist before birth seems extremely plausible. If being born at the right time conferred anything 'extra' then it cannot be a large part of the total inheritance. For example, children of induced births do not appear as alien within their own families (whereas this is occasionally noticed for adopted children within their host families). However, it would be unsound to dismiss the possibility of any advantage obtaining from an appropriately timed birth because such an effect could go unrecognized. If for example Gauquelin's athletes were even more outstanding as a result of being born at the appropriate time, this would be difficult to demonstrate. Provided that the effect is not negligibly small a statistical test would be possible for people born in this century — particularly in the United States because there is a great fashion for Caesarean sections there. The proportion of outstanding people in all spheres whose births were induced should be smaller than the proportion in a random sample of the population. I do not know of any research along these lines.

Mechanism

If advantage does result from appropriate timing then some mechanism must be involved. In Chapter 4 it was argued that metaphysical theories involving synchronicity or the cosmic loom encountered such difficulties that we are left with mechanism of some sort. The most likely mechanism would take the form of a stimulus emitted by the planet which impinges on some suitably sensitive organ of the foetus. The idea of an organ recalls the discussion of Chapter 3. The pattern of harmonics revealed a curious petal shape suggestive of an open flower receiving light (Figure 16). Now there is no corresponding physical organ with which to identify this petal pattern, but rather than dismiss the possibility, consider the implications if such a receptor exists. The separate petal groups could correspond to particular personality features and the stimulation of one specific group by a given planetary ray would colour that feature with its own particular quality. There is enough detail in such a postulated mechanism to contemplate the rest of the model that is implied. Its principal properties can be listed:

1. There is a pre-existing entity which possesses qualities and these qualities will ultimately manifest in the child and the mature adult. The qualities in the entity are related to an organ which has a flower-like structure incorporating groups of petals and the prominence of each group is correlated with the strength of the associated quality.

2. The entity responds to planetary stimulation at the moment of birth when there is a joining to the physical counterpart. The stimulation enhances the prominence of specific petal groups in ways which accord with the planet involved.

3. The planetary emanations may either reinforce the existing state of the entity or they may introduce a balancing effect by stimulating those groups not already prominent.

This is a rudimentary model in which no substance has yet been given to the means of stimulation. A likely candidate for the stimulating mechanism is resonance. One could envisage the petals in vibration and the effect of the planetary ray is to provoke increased vibration (provided that there is appropriate alignment of the planet with the 'petal'). Even with such a rudimentary model there is scope for explaining a number of separate elements of the evidence:

1.   The significance of the birth moment emerges as a simple consequence of there being a pre-existing entity and a time for linkage to the physical body. In traditional astrology, the birth time is considered as a symbolic moment corresponding to some special symbolic occurrence such as the first breath drawn by the baby or the first cry. No rationale has been offered for taking the first breath or cry — this has just become widely accepted, but actually it demands an explanation. If there is a close association between entity and physical vehicle happening at the time of birth and there is a special sensitivity to the planetary emanations at the same time then there is a very good reason for astrological effects to be associated with birth time.

2.   The fact that each of the Gauquelin distributions manifests harmonics which all repeat the same phase positions is explained by the need for any postulated organ of reception to be very similar in its construction as between one entity and another. The organs of the human body are very similar as between one person and another. The structure of receptor organs such as the eye and the ear is nearly identical among the whole human population. If we found the harmonic phases to be different for different groups then the argument for a standard receptor organ would fail; but the phasings are identical within the error levels to be expected in the data. It is clear that if there is a collection of entities with a sizeable proportion aiming for a specific planet's emanations to strike one of the three-group petals then the result will be a clustering of the planet's observed chart position near to each of the three petal directions. When an analysis is done of the collection of charts a prominent 3rd harmonic is exposed. The same argument applies if there is a proportion aiming for stimulation of the four-group of petals — there will be a clustering of the planet's observed chart position around each of the four petal directions — and a 4th harmonic will later be discovered in the distribution.

3.   One of the very striking facets of the Gauquelin evidence is the way in which the special distributions appear for the 'top' members of professional groups and not for those in more lowly ranks. The explanation for this is that the individuals of the elite groups are indeed out of the common run; i.e. the entities that pre-exist them have qualities that are unusual but, in addition, these entities seek birth times that result in enhancement of those qualities. Thus, the observed distributions reveal essentially the qualities that are already there (rather than being 'added' at the time of birth). Something is added at the time of birth but it seems to be a quite modest contribution and not readily detected from outward display. The Gauquelin elite groups are 'reinforcers' — their prominent planets correspond to the qualities that they already possess. This distinguishes them from 'ordinary people' who seek qualities that they do not already have.

4.   There may indeed be other people apart from members of the top professional groups who choose enhancement of their existing qualities. We do not yet know how to prove their existence by singling out a set of them and using statistical technique. However, the deliberate choice of specific kinds of planetary stimulation appears in the heredity evidence. An entity having 'chosen' suitable parents, thereby detemining to some extent his or her genetic endowment, also seeks similarities in the entity qualities. As a result we find children sharing the same prominent planets at birth as were prominent at the births of one or both parents.

5.   The points made above bring out the idea of purpose in aiming for a specific birth time. The astrological heredity evidence and particularly that part which indicates the possibility of thwarting attempts to be born at the 'right' time shows clearly that the foetus (or the entity) is striving for a specific time. What would be the point of such efforts? The model postulated suggests a quite definite purpose related to the life which follows — not accomplishing a symbolic conjunction at the birth time — but obtaining the

advantage of specific influences at the time when they are potent.

6.   There is a paradox which is baffling to many of those close to astrological research. On the one hand, as noted in Chapter 1, there is the abject failure of the 'Vernon Clark' type experiments in which astrologers attempt to pair up horoscopes with descriptions of the individuals to whom they apply. On the other is the experience well known to astrologers and to those contemplating their own horoscopes of discovering a parallel between the 'inner' aspirations of the subject and the astrological indications as shown by the natal chart. Given that the majority of people are aiming for qualities which are more than just the enhancement of those they already possessed (or which were possessed by the entity), the outward manifestation of their aspirations is usually far from obvious. On receiving suggestions that their inner aspirations are those indicated in the chart, people will often agree enthusiastically even though there is nothing in their overt behaviour to indicate the existence of such desires. Though this resolution of the paradox is satisfactory there are three caveats to bear in mind. First there is some doubt that traditional astrology is particularly accurate in delineating the inner aspirations (recall the contradiction between the traditional house meanings and the evidence of the Gauquelin 'houses'). Secondly there is the widespread human failing of accepting favourable portraits of one's character even when these are quite unrealistic. Finally there appears to be a pervasive latent desire to confirm the truth of astrology and many people abandon their normal critical faculties when assessing the accuracy of an interpretation.

7.   If there is an influence emanating from the planets and affecting receptors on earth, one would certainly be concerned if that influence travelled faster than the velocity of light. In fact, the analysis of the Gauquelin distributions given in Chapter 3 indicates clearly that the influence is travelling at the velocity of light, so no startling contravention of physical law is occurring. There is no

requirement that the planetary rays are electromagnetic or gravitational in character — any field effect must conform with the velocity restriction. There has been speculation recently deriving from the results of experiments on the spin of neutrinos that connections across the universe may exist that break the velocity of light rule. However, the experiments do not indicate any way in which a causal effect could be transmitted simultaneously, i.e. with infinite velocity.

8.   One of the awkward questions that astrologers face is the fact that non-identical twins bear little resemblance to one another despite being born close together in time (and at the same place!). This problem is usually met by arguing that the inevitable time delay between the two births results in slightly different charts and therefore different personalities. This is a difficult argument to sustain because the intervals between births of non-identical twins are not significantly different from those of identical twins and identical twins certainly do resemble one another markedly more than pairs of ordinary siblings. Waterhouse[1] in a study of over a thousand cases of twins found no significant difference between the time interval for monozygotic (identical) and non-identical pairs. Furthermore, studies of the interval indicate that 75 per cent of twins are born within an hour of each other. Thus there should certainly be more resemblance between non-identical twins than between siblings if the tenets of traditional astrology apply. However, it can be stated categorically that non-identical twins do not resemble one another any more than siblings. The reason for this strong statement is that numerous studies have been carried out on twins because of the strong resemblance which identical twins manifest. Apart from the obvious likenesses in appearance such twins also tend to suffer from the same illnesses (even when reared separately), have similar intelligence quotients and similar personalities. When statistics are brought to bear and the correlation coefficients for these similarities are measured, identical twins score much higher than siblings but non-identical twins have

much the same correlation coefficients as siblings. This is truly a difficult problem for traditional astrology, because it seems to imply that only genetic factors play any part in deciding the resemblances between members of the same family. If two of the children have exactly the same genetic source then indeed they resemble one another strongly but the fact that they were born at nearly the same time and place seems to have no bearing on the outcome since lacking that identical genetic source the resemblance fades right back to sibling level. The New Vitalism provides an explanation based on the same constraint effect noted for outside interference with the birth time. If two separate entities with different characteristics each seek appropriate birth times, and given the constraint that the interval between their births will be quite short, then the outcome must be that at least one of them is born at the 'wrong' time. This is simply a different kind of constraint from that introduced if there is surgical interference with the natural birth time. The ultimate effect of the constraint is not likely to be any more adverse than shifting birth time artificially but it does mean that seeking additional resemblances between dizygotic twins (over and above those found for siblings) because of nearly coincident birth times will fail. There is a further question which arises in considering monozygotic twins. If there are two pre-existing different entities involved, why are such twins identical? The answer is that in spite of their common genetic origin such twins, although having strong likenesses, differ in many respects of personality and tastes. In conventional explanations this has been put down to differences in upbringing and experience, but occasionally the personality differences are striking enough to strain credulity towards these explanations. The two pre-existing entities associated with monozygotic twins are similar but they are not identical.

9. If two children are born of different parents but at very nearly the same time and place, the problem of constraint discussed in the previous section does not arise. Both children could be born at the 'right' time. However, it does

not follow that 'time twins', as such children are called, will necessarily resemble one another strongly. Recalling the earlier discussion of the Gauquelin elite groups, it was pointed out that the majority of individuals do not choose birth times at which their latent characteristics will be reinforced. Reinforcement does occur for many of the elite groups, which is why they are detectable. It was suggested that others than those in the elite groups would also plan reinforcement but that they could not easily be discovered unless they had some common distinguishing feature. Given a more or less random distribution of 'reinforcers' in the population and also a fairly low incidence of such people it is possible to make one useful statement about time twins — which is that occasionally there will occur time twins who are reinforcers and when that happens the twins will resemble one another far more than a pair of randomly chosen people. It follows from this that one could expect some occasional but striking cases of time twins. This is indeed exactly what has been noted. Toonder and West[2] have made a useful collection of time twin cases and some of their instances (with full documentary evidence) are intriguing. However, the other side of the coin is just as important for supporting the model which is being proposed. There have been attempts to look for time twins in order to check the astrological assertion that resemblances between them should be seen. Gauquelin[3] searched among his large collection of notables to find suitable pairs where there was a small separation of the birth time. He could find nothing in common between the partners of such time pairings other than could be expected by chance. Dean[4] points out that in the last hundred years the Western countries should have produced more than ten million people born within one minute of each other and less than 15 miles apart. If there were a sizeable proportion of strongly alike time twins in the general population the researchers would have found them, but Dean quotes well-documented cases where there are no clear resemblances at all. The conclusion seems to be entirely in accordance with expectations derived from the model.

10. If the different characteristics exhibited by the Gauquelin elite groups arise from particular planets enhancing the activity of specific petal groups then it should be possible to separate an ostensibly homogeneous population into two or more sub-populations each of which 'belongs' to one petal group. Recalling that the harmonic and the petal group are two sides of the same coin because the detection of a set of one petal group involves the extraction of the corresponding harmonic from a distribution, the splitting of a population consists of identifying the characteristics associated with each harmonic. This is exactly what John Addey did when he split the Gauquelin athletes into two groups, as described in Chapter 3. He found that the Mars 3rd and 4th harmonics (both of which are strong for the athletes) referred to two sorts of athlete. The words used by biographers to describe the 3rd harmonic group were not the same as those used to describe the 4th harmonic group. Neither set of adjectives was actually inappropriate for athletes but it is clear that two different types are present. The 3rd harmonic could be said to reflect noble aspirations and the Olympic ideal, while the 4th is closer to the aggressive determination to win. The feat of separating the sub-populations is an impressive one and adds much weight to the case for the New Vitalism.

11. Although the evidence for the effectiveness of aspects is not as strong as that for planetary position in the diurnal circle, nevertheless there are some impressive collections. In Chapter 1 the work of Dieschbourg was described. Among astrologers agreement about the importance of aspects is universal. Now the angles between planets which are used as aspects are, in fact, divisions of the circle into an integral number of parts. Thus the trine corresponds to a division by 3, the squares and opposition to division by 4, the sextiles to division by 6, the semisquares to division by 8 and the semisextiles to division by 12. If two planets are separated by 120 degrees it follows that simultaneous stimulation of two of the petals corresponding to the 3rd harmonic of Figure 17 can occur. Similarly, if two planets are separated by 90

degrees then stimulation of two of the petals corresponding to the 4th harmonic can occur. It would be expected that the combined operation of two or more planets would have an increased effect compared with only one — and that the result would be an amalgam of the separate planetary qualities involved. This provides a very satisfactory link between the petal model and the planetary aspects — though it would be even more impressive if an inference from the model could be demonstrated to hold. Interestingly, there has been a piece of research carried out recently which appears to confirm the reasoning offered above. The separate harmonics (and in the model, the separate petal groups) seem to correspond to different areas of the personality or a different emphasis of the personality traits. Thus, for the athletes, the 3rd harmonic was associated with the noble Olympians and the 4th with the ambitious. What about the higher harmonics? What areas of personality or what special emphasis would correspond to a 5th harmonic? The recent research which could have a bearing on this question has been carried out on 'Eureka moments'. Kollerstrom and O'Neill[5] have investigated scientists who enjoyed a moment of pure inspiration when it seemed that the truth was suddenly revealed to them. Such moments are very rare (and are experienced by only a small number of scientists) but they are so unlike ordinary experience that there is no mistaking the occurrence. It has been suggested that creativity should be associated with quintiles and septiles (aspects obtained by dividing the circle into 5 and 7 respectively). The researchers examined all aspects in the charts of the scientists who had experienced a Eureka moment and found that quintiles and septiles were present far more often than would be expected by chance. They had only a modest collection of charts but the statistical significance of the result was 1 in 300 and there were further findings which suggest that this was not a freak result. Maybe the petal groups of five and seven (and beyond) correspond to more facets of personality.

12.   There is an area of astrology separate from interpretation of

natal charts and this is concerned with prognostication — attempts to indicate what is likely to happen in the future. There are a number of different ways in which astrologers go about this. Of all the methods used, most astrologers would agree that so-called 'transits' should be retained, even if they had to discard all other methods. An astrological transit is the passage of a planet or Sun or Moon over a zodiacal point which coincides with a 'sensitive' point in the natal chart. The sensitive point can be one of the angles (particularly Ascendant and MC) or one of the planets in the chart. The interpretation is based on the planet which is making the transit and on the point to which the transit is made. Thus a transit of one of the traditional 'malefics' (Mars or Saturn) over the Ascendant would be interpreted as a time when the subject was at risk from personal accident, whereas a transit of a traditional benefic (Venus or Jupiter) over the MC would be interpreted as a time when the subject could expect good fortune in his or her public life. There is great difficulty in designing a satisfactory test of the effectiveness of transits and there is no published test which demonstrates that transits 'work' in the sense of reaching significant statistical levels. Part of the difficulty derives from the fact that a variety of outcomes will fit the interpretation. Clearly there can be a host of ways in which you may have a personal accident and similarly a variety of types of good fortune in the public eye. However, the very fact that astrologers are nearly unanimous in averring that transits are effective suggests that with more ingenious tests there is a possibility that this widespread belief could be confirmed. If indeed the effectiveness of transits is proved then there is the problem of explaining how it occurs. The New Vitalism contains the presumption that the entity, pre-existing the embryo and associated with the physical body during its lifetime, is sensitive to the planetary rays (particularly at the moment of birth). The receptor organ or organs respond to rays from particular directions and the result is a stimulation of that 'petal' which is exposed. If it is conceded that the receptor organ continues to be sensitive to the rays after birth and throughout life then a possible mechanism of transit operation can be envisaged. Having a receptor organ is tantamount to carrying around a natal chart, in the sense that there are sets of sensitive spots arranged geometrically round a circle. Movements of planets over the sensitive spots could stimulate the receptor organ in a similar way to that occurring at the birth time. One could then expect the subject to manifest the particular qualities present in the entity to a more marked degree when the transit was occurring. Of course, this implies that the subject is generating his or her own accidents and own good fortune, which is not the interpretation usually offered by astrologers. Traditional astrology considers what the cosmos does to you as having as much importance as what you do to the cosmos.

The Planning Faculty

The model discussed above belongs in that general category referred to as 'vitalism' — the notion that human beings consist of a vital spirit contained within a physical body. For different reasons the idea of such a dualism has been advanced even by physical scientists. The biologist Hans Driesch[6] put forward the concept of 'entelechy' — an organizing principle which could co-ordinate the growth of the physical organism. Driesch found it incredible that all of the organization needed to build and sustain living organisms could derive entirely from the elementary building blocks of single cells. In contrast, the proposals in this chapter are advanced to explain the strange collection of evidence in the astrological field. It is appropriate to call it 'A New Vitalism'. There is no necessary contradiction between this vitalism and those which have preceded it. What has been called here the 'entity' might well possess the sort of properties which Driesch invoked for entelechy.

The preceding section has been concerned with the consequences of the New Vitalism — all of the effects which could be expected if it were true. There is still the earlier period before birth to be considered. Before the chosen birth time can materialize there must have been a planning operation. The planning involves two separate parts. First there must be the acquisition of knowledge about the area of operation (knowing where the planets are and where they will be in future time), and second there must be actual choice available. It seems unlikely that an entity could have much influence over the time of conception — it will be a matter of making the best choice within some restricted circumstances. However, this restriction will not matter much so far as the choice of time of day for the birth is concerned (the 'right place' in the diurnal circle). Adjustments in the final few hours will secure an appropriate planet in the chosen house. This is not so if certain other astrological features are sought. If it were desired to secure a solar aspect with one of the outer planets on the birthday then a shift of up to fifteen days might be necessary (taking all the aspects formed by multiples of 30 degrees between Sun and the planet). Even without any choice for the conception time this shift would not be out of the question. Variations of this order occur in the duration of normal pregnancies. The first requirement is to know the composition of the planetary scene.

If one considers the means by which information is gathered on the terrestrial plane there is a clear ordering of methods. The rule is to use the most direct method available. If you want to know about the weather then just looking outside is the first thing to do, only moving on to checking a barometer if necessary and perhaps consulting those who work with a huge model of the atmosphere to secure the best forecasts. This sequence applies in the animal kingdom. Homing pigeons fly to their lofts using visual clues as soon as they are within sight of home. Before that they appear to use any clues that are available. It has been discovered that they will navigate using the Sun when the weather is not cloudy. There is evidence that they are able to use the earth's magnetic field to assist their navigation (attaching small powerful bar magnets to them upsets their magnetic navigation).

It seems reasonable that something like visual clues could be available to the entity during some of the time that the planning operation is proceeding. If visual detection obeys the same sort of restrictions as apply on earth then there would be great difficulty in detecting the outer planets and for that matter also the planet Mercury.

The outer planets (Uranus, Neptune and Pluto) cannot be seen because they are distant and their light is faint. Mercury is difficult to see because its orbit is very close to the Sun and it is visible only in the morning just before sunrise and in the evening just after sunset. It is so elusive that most people have never seen it at all. Among all the Gauquelin findings it is quite striking that there are no results for Mercury, Uranus, Neptune and Pluto. Of course this does not mean that there are no emanations from these planets and no effects deriving from the emanations; it simply means that in terms of choosing and planning, only the readily detectable planets are likely to be considered. Now remembering that the Gauquelin distributions reveal what has been planned rather than what the planetary emanations actually affect, there is no reason to expect to find the 'invisible planets' showing up in the distributions. (Mercury is not 'invisible' in the same sense as the outer planets, and the reason for its absence in the Gauquelin findings may result from its being 'tied' to the Sun. This point is explained a little later.)

In the later stages of the planning operation, the entity is about to enter a close (and lifelong) association with the physical body. There could be difficulties during this phase of obtaining any immediate visual clues about the positions of the planets. The general rule about situations where the information flow is restricted is that the seeker turns to other methods. It seems likely that the entity in these later stages turns to a magnetic method of detection. Though there is a lack of final confirming evidence, it may be that Seymour's model of geomagnetic changes generated through magnetospheric tidal effects originated by the planets explains the way in which information about planetary position can be sensed. At any rate there is the strong evidence of the Gauquelin heredity findings, in which it was observed that parent/child prominent planet correlation was twice as high on geomagnetically disturbed days as on quiet days.

It could be objected that some of the evidence appears to suggest that the outer planets and Mercury do indeed play a part. The work of Dieschbourg was noted in Chapter 1. He found some solar aspects prominent to the point of statistical significance in some collections. For example Sun/Neptune aspects appeared more often than could be expected by chance in a collection of philosophers. The actual percentage deviation is small compared with the sort of shifts in the Gauquelin distributions — and that gives the clue. The Gauquelin results are for 'reinforcers' and do not, primarily, indicate the actual effects of the planetary emanations. The effects nevertheless do occur but are noticeable only weakly and it is necessary to select prominent practitioners for the slight excess of aspects above chance expectation to be observable.

Apart from Mercury and the outer planets, there is a further absence in the Gauquelin distributions, whether for elite groups or in the heredity findings. This absence concerns a very prominent heavenly body — the Sun. In traditional astrology, house position of the Sun is certainly considered important. However, one should be chary of attaching too much importance to such *ex cathedra* statements — recalling the Gauquelin demonstration that the traditional cadent houses are far from weak. The answer may well be that the Sun has a different role in the chart and its zodiacal position is relevant rather than its diurnal position. In Chapter 3 the results of research into the charts of poliomyelitis victims were given and it was the Sun's zodiacal position that emerged as the important factor. It is as if the diurnal circle were the second hand of the celestial clock and the zodiacal circle the hour hand. Perhaps there is another receptor for hour-hand factors. The twelve-fold symmetry of the polio distributions suggests a similar structure for the second receptor as for the first.

If indeed there is a special role for the Sun in the zodiac rather than in the diurnal circle, then there is an additional reason for failure to find Mercury located in the 9th and 12th houses at significant levels in the charts of professionals. Mercury has the smallest radius orbit of any of the planets. It stays within a small angular distance of the Sun (as viewed from earth). It follows therefore that if positioning the Sun in the zodiac is one purpose of the 'plan' then there cannot simultaneously be freedom to position Mercury in the diurnal circle — because it is effectively tied to the Sun's position. This argument applies with lesser force to Venus, i.e. the freedom to place Venus, once the Sun has been fixed, is restricted. It is interesting to note that Gauquelin only 'discovered' Venus as a planetary factor among his professionals some time after the initial analysis when he had moved on to studying personality traits. Venus is less prominent as a planetary factor: possibly for the reason advanced above — that freedom to place it is restricted.

Supporting Evidence

The basis of the New Vitalism lies in a a set of assumptions for which direct evidence is lacking. How plausible are these assumptions? Is it reasonable that a form of radiation emanates from the planets but has remained undetected by any scientific device? The answer depends on the sort of emanation which is being sought. It is incredible that any part of the electromagnetic spectrum is involved because this has been thoroughly explored over an enormous range of frequencies and the detection apparatus available is extremely sensitive. However, there is no special reason to confine the search to waves of the form most familiar to us. We are bombarded by vast numbers of particles which nearly all pass through us and indeed pass right through the earth and out of the other side as though we and the earth did not exist. These particles are neutrinos and they were discovered relatively recently. Interestingly enough they were postulated to exist because of the difficulty in explaining some kinds of interactions occurring among subatomic particles. Physicists are very unwilling to contemplate the breakdown of such fundamental laws as the conservation of mass/energy and the conservation of momentum, hence the need to postulate a new particle with zero electric charge (because conservation of charge is another fundamental requirement) and effectively zero mass but possessing angular momentum. After the intellectual leap needed to contemplate the existence of such shadowy particles they were found to be present in very large numbers, though their detection proved to be extremely difficult because so few of them interact with ordinary matter. The neutrino is a striking example of something which not only exists but also is omnipresent, interpenetrating all of space and matter yet unseen and almost undetectable. It is clear that after we have investigated the visible and tangible parts of the natural world our penetration of the invisible and intangible parts has to be through imagining possibilities which could explain anomalies — and then seeking evidence that those possibilites are real. The world of modern physics is full of waves and particles, most of which are quite invisible to us and moreover new notions are being added as each decade passes. The question to be asked is whether there could be emanations which currently lie outside of the world of physics.

Science looks askance at rays or waves which are neither vibrations in a medium nor electromagnetic in character, so what justification could there be for planetary rays which are detectable only by their effect on people? Well there is the phenomenon of telepathy — thought-transference between two people. This seems almost certainly not due to electromagnetic waves and yet it operates over long distances and does not appear to require much energy. Some sceptics doubt its occurrence and it is true that the story of research into extrasensory perception has been sullied by the occasional enthusiast who fakes results. However, there have been people to whom telepathy was commonplace — for whom it was unnecessary to devise elaborate and time-consuming experiments or calculate the statistics of correct guesses by the 'receiver' of transmitted thoughts. One such pair of people was the novelist Upton Sinclair and his wife. Over many years they performed hundreds of tests in which Sinclair transmitted a scene or an object and his wife attempted to draw a picture of what she 'picked up'. In a book, *Mental Radio*,[7] containing a collection of pairs of pictures — the transmitted and the received, the reader is invited to judge whether there has indeed been extrasensory transmission taking place. The pairs of pictures are fascinating because sometimes the receiver picks up a shape but not the idea behind it so the interpretation is ostensibly wrong but you know that the shape was received correctly. Sceptics can suggest that Sinclair and his wife constructed an elaborate fraud, but for what possible purpose? He was already a successful writer before this book was published. His novels were concerned frequently with the evils of capitalism and the desirability of socialism — nothing to do with occult abilities. It is quite possible that his reputation as a serious writer suffered when he was known to dabble in psychic matters. It seems to me that Sinclair offered a collection of evidence in order that people would give serious consideration to the possibility that extrasensory phenomena exist and that the world is a richer more mysterious place when you realize that. The Sinclairs were not unique; there have been other such 'sympathetic' individuals but most such people have no urge to publish their experiences (nor indeed the opportunity to do so). The kind of rapport that some pairs enjoy is material for anecdotes rather than systematic research and occasional rapport lends itself poorly to laboratory investigations.

The special organ which is sensitive to the planetary waves is a more demanding concept than the waves themselves. Although telepathy requires the existence of a detector for thought-waves, the organ postulated in the New Vitalism is required to be the actual source of particular qualities observed in the individual with whom it is associated. Moreover the organ must be a part of a pre-existing entity which becomes attached to the foetus at birth. The form of the organ is curiously unlike that of the sensory organs which are so familiar. The eye and the ear show little evidence of the stark geometry necessary for the flower organ. However, this kind of precise geometry is not uncommon in the natural world. Flowers and other plants can show precise geometric patterns and crystals reach a geometrical precision as high as one could wish. There is no problem about the formation of a geometrically structured organ, but rather why such a shape should come into being. The answer must surely be that all organs are adapted specifically to the nature of the emissions they are detecting. The eye has a lens in order that a clear image can be focused on the retina and the ear has a set of filaments to vibrate in resonance with incoming sound-waves. The planetary emissions all arrive from bodies which are in nearly the same plane — this sets clear guidelines for a receptor, which should have a planar form and be sensitive at its periphery.

If there is a receptor organ for the planetary waves, why are we not aware of the planets directly without the need for sight of them as they appear above the horizon? This question recalls the earlier discussion of telepathy. Only a relatively few people show telepathic ability to any marked extent. There is no obvious reason why this should be so. It has been suggested either that earlier less evolved humanoids may have possessed the ability and it has since atrophied, or alternatively that it is the sign of a more developed and emerging race. Whatever the truth about telepathy, the fact of its fairly thin occurrence prompts the thought that planetary awareness could be thinly spread or could have been enjoyed in the past and has since faded. If indeed there have been individuals who were directly aware of the planets this would meet the great difficulty that arises in trying to explain how astrology arose at all. The usual account suggests that astrology developed from noticing correspondences between appearances in the heavens and happenings on earth, gradually building up the whole scheme of signs, houses, planets and aspects. This explanation might have sufficed in the last century but if we consider the concentrated research that has been pursued during recent decades, it defies credulity. In spite of numerous attempts there is virtually no hard evidence for the signs. The only glimmer of hope comes from Smithers' work on very large samples, but even here the effect is small. Gauquelin tried hard to confirm the existence of signs and aspects without success. Dean records literally scores of trials attempting to match charts against personality inventories with results no better than chance. The only beacon in this landscape littered with research that failed to confirm traditional astrology using statistical methods is the Gauquelin work on top professionals. Unless the world today is quite a different place from the one inhabited by the early astrologers they would have had a monumental task in approaching the construction of the astrological edifice from first principles using only empirical guides to discover the characters of the planets and their potent positioning. They would have to guess correctly that only 'top people' would provide the necessary data for establishing the key planetary attributes and that diurnal position rather than zodiacal position was the relevant measurement. Any mistake along this rather narrow trail would have led to correlations at the chance level or rather to disagreement among the recorders and researchers about the 'real meaning' of the stars (assuming they were a priori convinced that there was truth to be discovered). From the viewpoint of the late twentieth century, the enterprise of establishing astrology from scratch by purely empirical methods looks incredible. However, if one or two of the early astrologers actually felt the vibrations of the planets and knew by direct perception that the nature of Mars was forcefulness and impulsiveness and energy then it would be possible to start assembling the astrological structure and seek for confirming instances. There are two further points that make this hypothesis even more likely. The first rests on the fact that out of the whole collection of assertions that comprises traditional astrology, the one set that stands out as completely confirmed by the Gauquelin work is that of the descriptions of the planetary qualities. Venus, Mars, Jupiter, Saturn and the Moon are indeed as you can find them described in the textbooks and as they were described long ago. Much of the rest of traditional astrology appears to have been embroidered round this main planetary thread by people who were not working through direct insight, as the early founders had done, but concerned with developing patterns and making, what seemed to them, logical extensions. The second point is that the early horoscopes were drawn up for rulers — kings and queens, but not for the common people. The rulers were the equivalent of Gauquelin's top professionals. There were far too few of them to provide the empirical base that would allow the building of astrology from scratch, but the early astrologers appeared to know that the manifestation of the planetary potencies was to be found in their kings and queens. Only later did the notion of drawing up charts for every Tom, Dick and Harry arise.

Vitalism

The sections above have suggested reasons why the notions of planetary waves and of receptor organs for those rays are not unreasonable. Every decade brings more of the invisible content of our universe to the surface of our comprehension and the idea of some more emissions (travelling at the velocity of light as they should) is plausible. However, the concept of the pre-existing entity goes beyond simple extensions of waves and receptors. It is not a novel idea — the 'ghost in the machine' is an old notion. In this century, vitalism of all kinds has receded before the advance of physics into biology. As the structure of DNA was deduced and the character of the genes described, so the ultimate secrets of life appeared to be emerging as special arrangements of the same old material substance. The rise of computing has stimulated this advance of mechanistic explanation. It seems an easy extension to relate the sequences of DNA to the code used in computers so that the term 'genetic code' has come into general use. The parallels with computing are persuasive and it is commonplace to hear of 'software' and 'hardware' replacing mind and brain. Because of this very persuasiveness of the language being used it is difficult to realize that there are some very large gaps in the explanations which are offered to account for phenomena such as the growth of organisms. It is hinted that the growth of organisms is genetically programmed, i.e. that the process is like feeding a program into a numerically controlled machine tool. However, a numerically controlled machine tool has a very elaborate array of interpretation devices to convert the signals coming from the tape into movements of the machine's parts. There is no evidence of the equivalent of such an array in living organisms. If we ask how an embryo consisting of a few cells starts to develop organs and limbs the answer is that instructions must be contained in the genetic program so that given enough time and effort by the researchers the connections between the program and the organism's development will be made clear. That important word 'must' is there because of the strong mechanistic premise from which the explanation starts. Evidence for believing in the genetic program theory depends on relating existence or absence of features in the developed embryo to existence or absence of specific gene groups — hence the rise of genetic engineering in which groups are deliberately introduced. However, there is a long way to travel between providing the builder with window frames, doors and bricks and getting a house. The fact that leaving out cables means no electricity supply or that substituting lattice windows changes the appearance is no argument for believing that the parts list is actually the house-building program.

The difficulties of accepting the current mechanistic theory of development led Sheldrake[8] to put forward his theory of morphic fields. He postulates that coexisting with the material world are fields having some similarities with the well-known electric, magnetic and gravitational fields. The morphic fields are the source of form in developing organisms. A herring develops herring-like form because there is a herring field already existing which influences that development. The herring field is modified by the existence over time of billions of herrings each contributing a little to the current herring field. Fields operate on behaviour as well as on development, so that all kinds of elaborate procedures such as courtship and nest-building, usually put down to 'instinct', derive from existing fields. Sheldrake[9] has recently extended the field concept to take in memory. He points out that attempts to associate memories with specific parts of the brain have had almost no success and that researchers have been driven to suggest that memories are in some extraordinary way distributed over the whole brain — somewhat in the same way as a hologram has the whole picture present in all its parts so that any fragment of the hologram can be used to re-create the picture (albeit somewhat less clearly than from the entire hologram). The hologram analogy fails for the same reason as the numerically controlled machine tool analogy — none of the extra apparatus needed is actually present. Because the morphic field concept for development and behaviour amounts to a huge cosmic memory bank, there is an internal logic about extending the idea to the local memories of individual creatures.

Whether or not Sheldrake's fields exist is less important than the way in which he has demonstrated flaws in the current theories of development, behaviour and memory. There are such serious defects in these theories that alternatives are necessary. The morphic field is one way of overcoming the defects but there are others as Sheldrake himself recognizes. In *The Presence of the Past*[9] he notes that the hypothesis he is putting forward could be translated into other terminologies. He offers as an extreme example of such another terminology the 'subtle bodies' and 'akashic records' of theosophy.[10] When one is formulating a new concept it is difficult to clothe it in enough detail to satisfy critics. Most of the description has to be about what it does rather than what it is. To account for development, an organizing principle is necessary along the lines of Driesch's 'entelechy'. Sheldrake has moved away from Driesch's explicit vitalism to the more distributed and less individuated notion of the field. This is not a radical departure. Alternatively the functions of organizing growth and development could be carried out by the entity of the New Vitalism.

The idea of a non-physical organ of reception is difficult to accept. One possibility which lends support to the idea is that the receptor organ corresponds to one of the 'chakras' to which clairvoyants often refer. It is said that there are seven separate chakras or psychic energy centres located at points within the physical body. These centres are described as each appearing like the spokes of a wheel — oriental seers use the pictorial analogy of the lotus. The individual chakras are considered to be associated with particular organs or functions of the body and the health of a person is reflected in the state of the chakras. These statements come from clairvoyants raised in different cultures and hint that there may indeed be psychic organs as well as physical organs making up the total human being.

The comments of clairvoyants necessarily carry little weight because they are usually not verifiable, but if we consider an entire system of medicine there is the body of evidence derived from successful treatments to be weighed in the scales. The ancient Chinese practice of acupuncture is enjoying increasing support in Europe and North America. There are two startling effects which the practitioners of acupuncture can demonstrate. The first is that of local anaesthesia. By simply inserting and stimulating a needle (usually in some unlikely location) remarkable unawareness of pain can be produced so that extensive operations can be performed on the patient in full consciousness. The second effect is that of alleviating or even curing certain chronic conditions such as arthritis. So effective has acupuncture proved to be that there is a body of orthodox medical practitioners in the UK who have trained in the practice and use it as part of their treatments. Now the interesting thing about acupuncture is that it is a system based on a theory of energy pathways in the human body — but these pathways have no physical counterparts as nerves or blood vessels. In other words the underlying basis of acupuncture is existence of psychic structures associated with the physical body. It is not as if the ancients were unaware of the physical organs and simply built their diagrams of energy flow to fit the outline of the body. The acupuncturists have an entire separate, coherent system — and the evidence of success suggests that the diagrams relate to real pathways even though we cannot see them.

Testing the Model

A scientific theory is a testable theory. From the statement of the theory it must be possible to devise tests which will distinguish between the theory and alternative explanations. This requirement applies to the New Vitalism as much as to any other theory. The devising of tests can be difficult because like so many phenomena from the field of psychical research, the actual occurrences are often elusive. If Gauquelin had sought for confirmations of the workings of astrology from charts of 'ordinary people' he would scarcely have thought it worthwhile to publish his findings — because the effects there are so weak. Only by using top professional groups was he able to show impressive results. It is rather as though the psychical researchers had discovered an infallible method of selecting talented sensitives — clairvoyants who could perform repeatedly to order.

Difficult as it is, the task of devising tests must be tackled and if possible, each test should probe different facets of the theory. In the following proposals, separate features of the New Vitalism are used as bases from which to develop predictions.

1. The receptor organ

The main characteristic of an organ is that its structure remains essentially constant and unvarying. One would not expect to find quite different sorts of ears or eyes among the members of some newly discovered tribe. It follows that one straightforward prediction can be made from the new Vitalism. If another group such as the Gauquelin top professionals is found for which one or more planets yields a distinctive distribution in the diurnal circle then a harmonic analysis will reveal that the phasing of the individual harmonics is materially the same as that found already for the Gauquelin groups. This is a quite general prediction and applies to any sort of group — not just professionals.

2. The enhancement effect

The Gauquelin results fade if individuals of lesser standing are included in the collections. This phenomenon is explained according to the New Vitalism by the difference between entities seeking reinforcement of their existing qualities rather than aspiring towards new and different qualities (possibly related to the genetic endowment they will acquire through their parents). The elite groups seek reinforcement; therefore, although the planetary effect is weak, these groups nevertheless show strong correlations between planetary position and personal characteristics. It has been suggested earlier that pairs of time twins who show striking similarities are also reinforcers. Hence a possible test consists of investigating the planetary positions at the birth times of strongly similar time twins. There should be the same correlation between diurnal planetary position and personal characteristics as were found for the Gauquelin professional groups.

3. Twins and constraints on birth time

The problems facing traditional astrology in explaining the differences between non-identical twins were discussed earlier in this chapter. The point is that non-identical twins do not resemble one another more than ordinary siblings whereas, unlike siblings, they are born very close together in time. According to the New Vitalism a special constraint arises when non-identical twins are born. The two entities are different and would, if they were seeking reinforcement of their existing qualities, choose different times to be born. However, because of the special constraint of their occupying the same womb, one or both of them is necessarily born at the 'wrong' time. This suggests a test of famous twins. Pairs of famous identical twins occur commonly enough for most people to have heard of them. In the sporting field there were the Bedser cricketing twins and in lawn tennis there are the Gulickson twins. There are also pairs of famous siblings — not necessarily in the same field. Julian Huxley was an eminent biologist and his brother Aldous was an eminent writer. If the New Vitalism explanation for astrological failure, in the case of non-identical twins, is sound, then it is possible to make a prediction about the chance of observing a pair of famous non-identical twins. If one of a pair of non-identical twins is famous for some special ability then the probability of the other twin also being famous is substantially less than in the case of two siblings. Thus if the frequency of occurrence of famous brothers or sisters of a famous person is measured it should come out higher than the frequency of occurrence of famous twins where the other (non-identical) is famous.

Extensions of the Theory

It was suggested in Chapter 4 that a good theory should be able to provide explanations for the hard evidence and also provide pointers to how the less well attested evidence could be accommodated within the same framework. In the sections below is sketched further potential for the New Vitalism in explanatory power.

1. 'Births' of ships

One of the fringe items, from the fourth tier of evidence listed in Chapter 4, was the traditional belief that charts drawn up for the launch of a ship or the signing of the constitution of a nation state could provide clear indications of the fortunes of each enterprise: as if the launch or the signing were in some way equivalent to a birth process. The New Vitalism contains the presumption that each human being has an associated psychic entity and that this entity is sensitive to the planetary emanations at the time of birth. Logically one could expect that all living things would have such entities associated with their physical forms. It has been suggested earlier that the growth and form of the physical vehicle derives from the entity rather than from some supposed genetic program. This implies that the manifestation of life on the physical plane stems from entities associating with matter. If an entity working through a body can generate physical form, then the possibility arises of entities being the source of psychic forms. If one contemplates the building of a ship it is apparent that much mental and physical effort go into it. The ship lives as a concept in the minds of its designers and in the minds of all those engaged in its construction. A long period of close mental focus on the form of the ship takes place. During this time there could be the formation of a ship psychic entity. At the time of a ceremony to mark the ship's launch it could be expected that this entity would attach itself to the ship and the association would occur when there was particular sensitivity to the planetary emanations. If these suppositions are correct then an astrological chart for the ship would not be so absurd as it might seem at first sight. A similar formation of a psychic entity could occur whenever there is a concept held in common by many people and its materialization in physical form may be the occasion for some influence from the planetary rays.

2. The Kolisko experiments

It has been argued above that all living creatures should be associated with psychic entities. This was a logical extension from the requirement that human beings consist of physical envelope and entity. However, there is no *a priori* case for excluding the inorganic world. One would hardly expect anything as complex as that needed for living creatures but something simple could be envisaged for individual chemical elements. If this is true then particular elements should be affected by the planetary emanations. Clearly it is not a strong effect, otherwise we would have noticed it in many instances, but given a context in which the element is finely poised and a particular physical or chemical change could go either way we might expect that the astrological effects would show themselves. Maybe the Kolisko experiments did reveal the planets affecting inorganic materials.

3. Fate

Whereas the Gauquelin findings concern profession and also personality characteristics, traditional astrology has been at least as much concerned with 'good fortune' and 'bad fortune'. It seems a far cry from saying that someone is buoyant and cheerful to saying that he or she is 'lucky', i.e. that circumstances conspire to bring fame and fortune. Of course there is one sense in which the Gauquelin elite groups must have enjoyed a more than generous slice of luck. Great success in this world depends on more than just ability and application. Being in the right place at the right time and being noticed by the right people certainly count if you are an aspiring politician. The basis of the New Vitalism is the concept of an entity choosing a physical vehicle and to some extent choosing a time which either enhances existing qualities or seeks to complement them. Some of the choices made imply a consciousness of a higher order than that found on the physical plane. Ordinary human beings do not obviously show access to such superior powers. It seems as though putting on a physical garment dulls awareness. However, the power of the entity to know the 'right' time for action is doubtless still present. When our 'lucky' aspirant to high places inexplicably does just the right thing and moves up another rung of the ladder we can put it down to chance or to some guiding sixth sense. The New Vitalism implies that the aspirant's entity does have a real sixth sense and can influence choice (without the recipient being aware of it). It seems unlikely that this beneficient power is confined to the Gauquelin elite groups. When the astrologer forecasts good fortune for a client at a specific time, what is being attempted is a prediction of when the entity will be stimulated by the planetary emissions to 'choose' wisely. Astrologers do not necessarily get such predictions right. What is being argued here is the process by which 'good fortune' and its forecasting could come about. The query could naturally be raised of what source produces bad fortune. Because it raises several other issues this question is reserved for the next chapter.

Gaps in the Theory

In order to have a balanced view of a theory it is necessary to consider its failures as well as its successes. The New Vitalism accounts for nearly all of the hard evidence and much of the evidence which is of lower quality. However, there are gaps and these are considered below:

1. Source of the planetary qualities

The spectrum of electromagnetic waves is well understood. We know that vibrating electrons emit waves and the properties of those waves are a function of their frequency. Those of low frequency (radio waves) carry long distances and can penetrate all kinds of non-conducting matter. At the higher frequencies there are waves to which the retinas of our eyes are sensitive — the visible waves, and at still higher frequencies are X-rays and gamma rays. All aspects of generation, transmission and detection of all these wavebands are known in detail. In contrast, the source of the planetary qualities, as revealed in the personal characteristics of the individuals who have them prominent at their times of birth, is a mystery and the New Vitalism sheds no more light on it. Because the receptor organ is psychic in nature and the emanations affecting it are also psychic, we can infer that it is not the physical planet which is responsible for the emanations. One could suppose that the source of the emanations is an entity associated with the planet in the same way as a human entity is associated with the human body. However, this is only supposition and makes no progress in accounting for the separate and distinct qualities of each of the planets.

2. Prognostications from directions

Traditional astrologers use other methods of prognostication in addition to transits which have already been discussed. These methods are based on symbolism. Thus one may 'progress' the chart forward through the days which follow birth in order to see how the chart changes and note the significance of those changes (e.g. aspects closing to exactitude). Then the principle of 'a day for a year' is applied, so that what was seen in the natal chart progressed to the twentieth day would apply to the twentieth year of the subject's life. There is no particular rationale for the 'day for a year' rule — it is something which has been handed down to us as part of astrological lore. Such methods of prognostication have probably received less attention (in terms of investigating the truth of them) than transits. It has to be said that the evidence for them is anecdotal; if indeed they 'work' then the New Vitalism offers no mechanism by which their operation could be explained.

3. Diurnal circles and physical circles

There is a problem about the diurnal circle which Gauquelin has used to define his sectors. He employs a time division to set the sector boundaries. If those boundaries are set out along the ecliptic circle they are not, in general, evenly spaced. Moreover the MC which is always a quarter of a circle away from the Ascendant in Gauquelin's circle, is often much more or much less than 90 degrees from the Ascendant if measured along the ecliptic. The Gauquelin circle is not a physical circle and therefore angles measured in it do not necessarily correspond to angles measured in any physical circle. The New Vitalism requires that receptor organs have consistent geometry — in other words they must use circles in which the angles are not varying with the time of day and season of the year. It may be that a particular physical circle would show up the harmonics of the Gauquelin distributions better than those found in the diurnal circle. I have experimented with the prime vertical, which is a physical circle having four points (the angles) in common with the Gauquelin circle. However, if one sets out each of the distributions in the prime vertical, the amplitudes of the harmonics are not any larger nor are the phases of the harmonics from different distributions more closely clustered. I conclude that the prime vertical is not the correct circle to use, and the question is still open. This is not so much a failure of the New Vitalism as a minor defect.

4. Orientation of the receptor

In order for the planetary emanations to strike the receptor organ at its periphery and stimulate the appropriate petal groups, it must be orientated correctly. The question arises of how this orientation is carried out. In the physical body there are in-built mechanisms for orientation so that one can sense the upright position and departures from it. Within the ear is a wonderfully sensitive device for carrying out these functions. However, the newborn baby is not in any special orientation, and it is not clear how any receptor organ could be accurately set. This remains as a wholly unexplained feature of the theory.

5. The 'Great Year'

There is a collection of ideas in astrology that go well beyond the interpretation of natal charts. For example there is the 'Great Year' of 26,000 years during which the precession of the equinoxes carries through a whole circle. An equinoctial point is seen to move slowly through the constellations, taking all of the great year to pass through the twelve signs (as defined by the constellations). Each sign takes about 2,000 years and it is supposed that passage through a sign correlates with the character of the age. Thus, we are now moving from the Piscean Age into the Aquarian Age. If this is indeed true then the explanation must be sought elsewhere than in the New Vitalism. A similar position applies to so-called 'horary astrology.' It is supposed that the moment of asking some important question is significant in the sense that a chart set up for that moment will contain elements which can be interpreted as an answer to that question. Again there is no obvious way in which the New Vitalism can assist in explaining such things.

These are some of the gaps in the theory. It is likely that there are others and no doubt there are critics who will be willing to point them out. However, the general case appears sound enough to draw some implications and these are considered in the next chapter.

6
THE MESSAGE OF ASTROLOGY

Recapitulation

It was argued in Chapter 4 that existing theories have serious defects which make it necessary to consider new models for astrology. The biggest problem for 'trigger' theories entailing a physical stimulation to the foetus via magnetic fields or similar mechanism is that an extended planning operation is necessary to achieve birth at a particular time, whereas the trigger condition lasts only a short time. Once a planning process is accepted it makes sense to consider external effects which could interfere with that planning and Gauquelin's heredity findings when there has been interference by drugs or surgery illustrate very clearly that the planning intention can be upset. Given a pre-existing entity responsible for the planning then it is possible to contemplate the entity's possession of specific characteristics and that provides an explanation for one of the most striking aspects of the Gauquelin work. Only top professionals show the typical distributions in the diurnal circle and if such individuals indeed possess prior characteristics which are enhanced by choosing a birth time reinforcing those characteristics then this would distinguish them sharply from others who seek complementary qualities through their birth time choices.

Those are the central arguments for the New Vitalism. They are supported by points deriving from other studies. In particular the results of harmonic analysis on the diurnal distributions show that individual harmonics from the separate professional groups and separate planets have identical phasing implying a universal receptor organ for the entity in a similar way to the universal organs of sound and light reception which are familiar to us as ears and eyes. The twins paradox is resolved and it is no longer necessary to invoke tiny birth time differences between non-identical twins.

Difficulties with Vitalism

In spite of the explanatory power of the New Vitalism there is a central difficulty which has faced all proposals for vitalistic theories. If the vital spark is truly immaterial then how can it possibly influence the physical brain and body? Alternatively, if the spark is really only an aspect of the physical form then why is it not detectable in the same way that all the intricacies of the body's organs yield to physical investigation? If indeed the choice is as stark as that then the case against vitalism is inalienable. However, there are features of scientific investigation which suggest some interesting 'half-way' stages between completely immaterial and completely physical.

Radio waves are not detectable by our unaided senses. They pass readily through solid objects without apparently affecting them at all. Indeed they have a sort of ghostly existence and their curious status would be a source of wonderment except that they have become familiar and commonplace. Radio waves could have been there all around us, interpenetrating our world without our having the slightest notion of their existence. Indeed they were there all around us because their emission does not depend on specially built transmitters. Until a sensitive receiving device had been constructed there was no way of developing the technology of radio communication. Radio waves already existed because they are emitted by other sources. For example every flash of lightning emits a strong burst of radio waves. Radio waves are not thought of as non-physical because they clearly interact with physical material in a way that is susceptible of experiment. Hertz in his first experiments showed that the waves could be reflected and refracted by suitable materials. Instead of thinking of radio waves as non-physical it is convenient to regard them as more subtle manifestations than the everyday world of tables and chairs.

Once a gradation of subtlety is accepted then it is a short step to considering the possibility of an entity which is subtle enough to escape the present range of our detection instruments but does nevertheless interact with a living creature. It would be surprising if absolutely no physical detection (in the sense of a piece of apparatus as a detector) could be devised. If the entity can interact with a brain then it must be able to interact with other material constructs — it is just that suitable methods have not yet been devised.

Survival

If the nature of the entity is a subtle form of matter that pre-exists the body then it would seem very likely that it survives the dissolution of the body at death. There is no direct evidence from astrology that would suggest this; it is just a logical inference from the indications of pre-existence. If the entity can exist without a body before birth then it would seem entirely reasonable that it can exist without a body after death. Although there is no direct evidence from astrology to support this contention, there is indirect confirmation from the idea of planning which is one of the central tenets of the New Vitalism. If the entity plans, in the sense of making attempts to ensure that birth occurs at an appropriate time, one can reasonably ask what objectives are being sought. It seems straightforward in the case of the 'top people' for whom the objective could be labelled 'success', and therefore related to this life, but what is to be assumed about lives which are not in any recognizable sense successful? There are various possible answers to this question. For example, the plans could have gone awry, or there may be a different criterion for success, or success is not a universal goal. Here the search for planning objectives is relevant, because one cannot argue simple extensions from Gauquelin's groups of professionals. If groups of top athletes, of top writers and of top politicians each show striking distributions of particular planets in their natal charts, why not top criminals? This is of particular interest because it could be supposed that the groups of top people considered by Gauquelin share a quality of public visibility — perhaps more important than any other qualities. This public visibility is shared by some criminals (though the term 'notoriety' is perhaps more apposite).

One of the first investigations pursued by Gauquelin concerned notorious criminals, but he found no planetary distribution characteristic of criminals. From this result it can be safely assumed that entities do not plan for success in crime. This sheds some light on the criteria which guide the planning but there is a further relevant finding. In Chapter 2 it was noted that the first analysis conducted by John Addey and myself concerned the distribution of the Sun in charts of poliomyelitis victims. We found a clear pattern of harmonics which was confirmed in a second sample. This finding opens up a new perspective on the objectives of the entity. Could there actually be planning for some crippling illness? This seems a very unlikely proposition but it would be inconsistent to maintain that the entity knows enough about the consequences of using a particular body in cases of achieving 'success' but is ignorant if a sort of failure is in prospect. However, this inconsistency is avoided if it is recognized that constraints operate on the plane of the entity as much as they do on the earthly plane. We are accustomed to sympathizing with a child doomed to some inherited disability — constrained by its physical frame. At a different level we could sympathize with the entity constrained to choose such a vehicle.

These aspects of planning and the criteria of the planner suggest a wider horizon than the limits of an earthly life. What could be the point of accepting a constraint such as poliomyelitis unless there was more to come? Similarly, the lack of planning for a criminal career suggests that success in purely materialist terms is not a criterion and that training for the longer term is a better description. Although the astrological case for pre-existence is stronger than it is for survival, the points listed above offer support to the belief that there is life beyond the grave.

Religion

So much of the material discussed above is reminiscent of central beliefs in the great religions of the world that it would seem curious if no reference were made to the parallelisms. The account of the entity built up from astrological indications is very close to that of the soul or spirit in Christianity. The concept of pre-existence is a necessary part of those religions such as Buddhism which have reincarnation as a part of their doctrine. The constraints to which the entity is subject are recognizable as the karmic debts which figure in religions teaching reincarnation.

The term 'beliefs' implies that there is no evidence for the truth of these propositions, but in recent times there has been substantial relevant research effort with some notable successes. Because of the power of modern medicine to keep people alive who in former times would have died, many individuals have 'come back' literally from death's door. Resuscitation from a state of apparent death occurs quite frequently. Some of those who have experienced this state of near death report that they had appeared to have consciousness outside of their physical bodies; they could look down on their bodies from a point somewhere near the ceiling. Some accounts refer to travelling in this out-of-the-body state along a tunnel towards a bright light and emerging into a heavenly landscape. Enjoyment of the post-death state ceases as they are 'told to return' or are rudely pulled back as vigorous resuscitation is applied.[1]

The rising number of near-death experiences cannot be regarded as proof of survival because we know that people *in extremis* suffer from all sorts of delusions. However, what is interesting about the accounts is the degree to which they conform to a single pattern, unlike the fantasies of those who are deranged. The same floating above the physical envelope, journey along the tunnel and intense light at the end turn up repeatedly. The one area of the experience which could provide a check on its authenticity is the viewing by the discarnate entity of the hospital room and activities of medical staff during the near-death phase. Memories that the individual retains of this phase after revival should correspond to the actual happenings around the 'corpse'. Research which has been directed towards discovering whether such memories are sound indicate that they are.[2] Resuscitated individuals have knowledge of what was going on in a large area around them during a period when they were effectively dead.

Given that there may be some evidence for survival, it is still difficult to accept the idea of pre-existence simply because most people do not have any memories of a prior existence. There have always been stories of those who could remember former lives but the evidence has been mixed and not entirely convincing. However, more recently there has been a concerted effort to collect evidence from young children who spoke of their immediate past lives. Stevenson's[3] work is the best-known. Such cases have tended to occur in countries such as India where there is a tradition of belief in reincarnation and children recounting alleged past experiences receive a sympathetic hearing. Checking a child's account of a past life, particularly if it is supposed to have taken place recently and near to where the child is living, is relatively easy. All kinds of circumstantial detail can be used and the possibility of fraud is very slight because the entire experience of a small child is so limited. Thousands of such cases are now on record.

The second line of inquiry on pre-existence lies in hypnotic regression. Under deep hypnosis some subjects allegedly can be carried back in memory not only to early childhood but even to before this time so that they relive past lives and the periods between lives. Of the investigations that have been described, those of Whitton[4] are of particular interest because some of his subjects report encounters with a group of advisers whose role is to assist the planning of a soul on the brink of incarnation. If the hypnotically obtained past memories of Whitton's subjects are to be believed then souls do indeed plan their future lives and are accorded assistance in so doing. Whitton is a therapist who has taken a special interest in patients whose traumas derive not from early experiences in this life but from experiences prior to that. There is no doctrinal source for this concept of planning a life — indeed Whitton's subjects come from an agnostic or orthodox Christian background — unlike people within the Eastern religions where emphasis on reincarnation is commonplace. Nor would one expect Whitton himself to have invented such a concept and successfully impressed it on his patients. Even though there can be little prospect of obtaining 'hard evidence' of a real planning operation prior to birth, the material collected by Whitton provides a strong pointer to the likelihood of its reality.

There is one other facet of religious teaching about the soul which is relevant to the New Vitalism. Again from the East comes the concept of special psychic energy centres associated with specific parts of the physical body. As mentioned in Chapter 5, these centres are termed 'chakras' and each chakra is said to look like a wheel or the petals of a lotus flower. This belief is interesting because it offers a possible source for the receptor organ which has been proposed as the receiver of planetary emanations. The particular requirement of this organ is that it should be geometric in design corresponding to the harmonics discovered in the diurnal distributions of planets from collections of natal charts. Indeed the harmonics set out as radical spikes prompted the term 'flower' to describe them.

Though the support offered by clairvoyants, hypnotists and traditional religion is not being put in the scales along with the hard statistical evidence, it is indicative that the New Vitalism is worthy of serious attention. The theory not only offers explanations for a number of apparent contradictions among the wealth of evidence, but also suggests a range of points that could be called 'messages'.

The Astrological Message

The New Vitalism provides explanations for several paradoxes of astrological research and it also offers some clear messages of guidance on the personal and the general plane. The first points concern astrological practice:

1. Dean has collected the results of numerous tests in which astrologers attempt to match people with their charts. The results are consistently at the chance level. Furthermore it seems that astrologers do not even agree among themselves; i.e. in choosing a wrong match they find different wrong matches, so that there is not even consistency among astrologers. The answer to this stream of apparent failure is that people in general do not manifest the qualities that are indicated in their natal charts to any marked extent. Choice of birth time is indicative of the soul's aspirations and its intended relationship with the physical world. Only in cases where the intention is an enhancement of characteristics is there any straightforward connection between the chart and personality traits. Professional astrologers may succeed in establishing rapport with their clients and interpreting their inner aspirations. It seems likely that an element of psychic insight is involved for this to be successful. How else

are we to explain the apparent lack of agreement among astrologers faced with a 'mechanical' process of chart matching. A similar difficulty arises in explaining the variety of emphases on different facets of the chart. Among astrologers there is adherence to different house systems, to different zodiacs (tropical and sidereal) and to different orbs for the aspects. Finally, there are differences in the importance which individual astrologers attach to the separate indications of the chart. Yet in spite of this bewildering variety, some professional astrologers do establish the necessary rapport and provide a service which is useful to the client.

2.   The second point follows on from the first. Given that rapport is necessary for there to be a useful outcome in an astrologer-client relationship, all 'newspaper' astrology and schemes for the mechanical churning out of charts with interpretations by feeding in dates are useless. Astrology is very old and there is a widespread glimmering of awareness in the psyche that 'there is something in it'. Newspaper proprietors, popularizers and unscrupulous hucksters can cash in on the subtle fascination of astrology. This is unfortunate because it deters those who might otherwise be serious students.

3.   Only a small part of traditional astrology has received confirmation through the exacting process of statistical testing. However, the results over the last few decades are so impressive that further research is well justified. It is interesting that attempts to confirm traditional astrology have been notably unsuccessful, but when researchers have thrown the net wide and been prepared to look for 'anything that is there' the results have been rewarding. If Gauquelin had stuck to checking traditional astrology, progress would have been slow indeed. Now the need is for the same kind of flair and perseverance which he demonstrated, but applied to other areas. It would be very surprising if there were absolutely nothing in the traditional belief that astrological prediction is possible. However, I doubt that investigations of the traditional forecasting techniques will

be fruitful. I say this because in the early 1950s I collaborated with Margaret Hone (one of the founders of the Faculty of Astrological Studies) in devising an experiment to check the effects of transits on a group of subjects. An astrological transit occurs when a planet comes to the same point in the sky as some sensitive point in the natal chart. The sensitive point may be one of the angles (Ascendant or MC), a house cusp or a planet. The character of the event associated with the transit should reflect the nature of the planet and the particular point in the chart to which the transit is made. In order for the experiment to exclude bias we arranged for the subjects to keep diaries rather than to ask them what had happened at some special time. Having calculated all the transits which had applied, it was necessary to compare the diary entries for those periods when transits should have been 'active'. Although one would not expect a large number of striking events during the months of our trial (by definition a striking event is a rarity) nevertheless there should have been a few cases of interest because of the size of our group. Indeed there were, and some people suffered accidents, at least one subject moved house and so on. I have to report that the correlation of events with transit indications was so poor that we were discouraged from continuing the exercise. I do not conclude from this outcome that prediction cannot occur. I think it more likely that a different kind of experiment is needed. Perhaps that special population of 'top people' would be appropriate subjects.

The Personal Message

Although the astrological findings are striking, it is my own view that the personal message for people living today in the turbulent later years of the twentieth century is more important. Statistical research has demonstrated that parts of traditional astrology are almost certainly true. Whereas some degree of credence is conferred by anecdotal evidence, the power of replicated tests with large samples is overwhelming, particularly where the samples are drawn from data generally available and not confined to particular laboratories or special staff. Similarly, the large collection of cases suggesting pre-existence is suggestive but it is not conclusive, whereas the astrological heredity data including cases of 'interference' is explicable only by postulating a planning entity — conveniently called 'soul'. In today's climate of materialism, it will take more than a collection of statistics on birth times and a logical argument to convince everyone that the soul is a reality. However, the implications of pre-existence and survival are profoundly liberating in the same way that studies of astronomy and geology are liberating. Realization of the vastness of time and space frees one, if only momentarily, from the narrow confines of everyday existence. Listed below are some of the relevant consequences stemming from the 'soul concept'.

1.   The immediate consequence of the notion of planning a birth time — and indeed a life — is simply that you chose to come here. Clearly your consciousness at the time of choosing was on a higher plane and taking a longer view than the limited consciousness being used to consider this proposition. Your reasons for coming may not be apparent and the source of the constraints which you have to endure may be quite obscure, but realizing that the choice was made gives you quite a new viewpoint. Life is not: '. . . a tale/ Told by an idiot, full of sound and fury,/ Signifying nothing.'[5] You, at a mundane level, may feel without purpose, but you at the soul level have enough purpose to accept earthly life with all that it brings.

2.   Apart from the wider horizons that come with acceptance of soul, there are some very practical consequences. The skills you acquire, the disciplines you accept are not lost as you pass from this plane; they are a part of your enduring self. The child prodigy manifests skills acquired in the past and now being 'remembered'. The survival of acquired skills has relevance for those inclined towards idleness with advancing age. 'Why bother, it will soon all be over' is a common thought but inappropriate when the truth of survival is accepted.

3.   It was noted earlier that the planning extends even to lives

that will involve acute suffering (the poliomyelitis victims) and this puts quite a different significance on life's afflictions. We are accustomed to thinking of illness as 'bad luck' or as knowledge advances of 'poor genetic inheritance' or 'unhealthy environment'. So deep does this idea of bad luck go that most people enduring a particularly outrageous piece of ill fortune will ask bitterly: 'Why me?' It seems likely that the seeds of many of the constraints we endure have been sown in the past. The memories of those seeds have (thankfully perhaps) faded but the fruits are all too present.

4.   The idea of seeds that can be the source of future constraints has its corollary in the notion of seeds that can be the source of opportunities. The child prodigy reaps the harvest of past investment and no doubt all the gifts that you can leave to posterity will return to you as 'good luck'. Planting trees will not only prevent soil erosion, encourage a micro-climate and stave off the carbon dioxide problem, it will also create a pleasant landscape for you to walk through when you return here.

5.   This is an era when the religion of success is acceptable: 'What is good for General Motors is good for America.' Slowly the consequences of a creed which sets most store by ambition and acquisition are becoming apparent. Economic success has terrible effects on our ecosystems. Similarly, a personal creed of acquisition has unpleasant side-effects. If this little existence were the whole story there might be some justification for grabbing as much as one can, but with wider horizons there is the realization that what is happening here is, above all, a learning process. You cannot carry away your cash and your worldly assets, but you can graduate to the next stage — you can be a better human being.

The Social Message

One of the extraordinary things about religion is the way in which religious people in all countries and in all ages have been able to separate their own virtue and their own salvation from that of their fellows. We have had the spectacle of very noble sentiments accompanied by the most cruel behaviour towards groups of people who were not of the same persuasion. Much of what has been stated in the foregoing section about personal attitudes could be found in one or other of the better-known religious texts. However, the general points to be derived from consideration of the new evidence go well beyond the texts. The first of the social messages listed below carries strong theological overtones though it is really not a *cause célèbre*.

1.   Some religious groups consider contraception and abortion to be sins. The reasoning is that these practices are 'unnatural' and, in the case of abortion there is the destruction of life. The New Vitalism suggests that souls seek available vehicles for their incarnation and furthermore that the total union of body and soul is not achieved until birth occurs. It follows that the abortion of a foetus represents a thwarting of the plans made by a soul seeking incarnation. This is hardly a sin on the grand scale and certainly does not justify the intense campaigns mounted by anti-abortion lobbyists. None the less the abortion of a healthy foetus is 'unnatural' and can cause trauma and guilt feelings in the mother (or even injury if it is botched). In addition, there may be excellent reasons for the selection and timing of the soul attempting incarnation. For these reasons, abortion is not to be undertaken lightly. (For someone living in the West, the information that abortion is used as one of the principal methods of birth control in some of the countries of Eastern Europe evokes feelings at least of distaste and even of horror.)

2.   There is a current of revolt starting against 'high-tech' births. Mothers-to-be are taking more and more interest in 'natural' childbirth. Instead of allowing control of the timing to be in the hands of (usually male) medical experts, pregnant women are asserting their right to choose the manner and timing of their parturition. In the Netherlands, the number of home births is rising vigorously. Pregnant women are objecting to being labelled as patients, i.e. as people who are ill and therefore have forfeited their rights to decide

treatment in favour of the experts. This is in many ways a welcome sign. Experts in the fields of technology and medicine have committed follies on the grand scale and there is plenty of evidence to suggest that instinct is a good guide to the breeding and rearing of the young — as it clearly is in the case of the animal kingdom. The New Vitalism suggests a further reason for the reintroduction of natural childbirth. Souls attempt to achieve particular timings for the births of their earthly shells. There is no way in which we can yet measure the value derived from a well-timed birth. However, it would seem wise to be cautious in this matter, and proceed on the assumption that the time of birth occurring without any outside interference (through drugs or surgery) is one that is beneficial, in the sense of being appropriate to the newborn.

3.   Recently there has been recognition of the fact that so-called 'development' activity, principally in Third World countries, destroys topsoil, fresh water, atmospheric systems and genetic resources. This recognition has reached as high as the Vice-President of the World Bank for policy, planning and research. In March 1988 he gave a speech[6] in which he explained that he had been asked to sign a document which would result in the bank approving a scheme in South Asia for irrigation without drainage. The added cost of drainage would fail the bank's test of 10 per cent return on investment. He was thus faced with a dilemma. As he put it: 'The accepted economic justification for proceeding with the investment was certain to lead to a degrading of the resource base, and there was no acceptable justification for protecting those resources from destruction.' In other words, he recognized the destructiveness inherent in the project, but found himself obliged by the constraints of the bank's costing system to endorse it despite this.

    In order to understand why intelligent men acting in good faith will commit follies of such enormity, it is necessary to understand the basis on which projects are assessed. A balance sheet is constructed with all costs entered on one side and with all benefits (expressed in monetary terms) on the other. Provided that the benefits exceed the costs the project is deemed worthwhile.[7] In order to cope with the distribution over time of both costs and benefits a discounting technique is used. If a cost is incurred in five years after the commencement of the project its size is reduced in the balance sheet to that sum, which if invested now, would yield the requisite sum after five years. This 'discounted cost' is referred to as the 'present cost' or more usually as the 'present value' because costs and benefits are considered as just the positive and negative elements of overall value. Similarly all other costs and all benefits are discounted so that whatever their distribution in time they are all brought to the same measure of present value. It is relatively easy to justify discounting procedure in the case of a cost because it is clear that a cost incurred in n years time is effectively less than one incurred now. You can indeed put a smaller sum into investment so that the required amount will be available in n years time. It is rather more difficult to justify the discounting of future benefits (particularly where these are of a non-monetary character) and appeal has to be made to observed behaviour. People behave as if a benefit in the future were less valuable than if it were available now. Then for consistency one should clearly discount benefits at the same rate as one discounts costs. It is argued that the appropriate discount rate is that which is typically on offer as return on investment. This level will also be reflected in the interest rate being charged by banks on loans. Firms subject to 'capital rationing' may require higher discount rates for their projects. However, the typical discount used by governments and international agencies is of the order of 10 per cent p.a.

In order to appreciate the effect of a 10 per cent discount rate it is useful to think of the value of £1 if it is received in n years time. If it is received in seven years it has halved and is worth 50p. After forty years it is down to 2p and after a hundred years down to 0.007p. To put it another way the present value of £1 received in a century's time is 14,000 times less than receiving it now. As a result of this rapid decline in present value as time passes, the more distant costs and benefits are effectively written off the balance sheet. There are well-known quotes from leading economists to justify this result: 'Why should I care about posterity; what has posterity ever done for me?' and Keynes' more pithy 'In the long run we are all dead.'

There is a further problem associated with the balance sheet approach. Benefits which are not marketable are not usually put into the balance sheet at all. Thus damage to natural ecosystems, where this does not immediately affect agricultural land, is not noted; neither is interference with climatic systems or loss of genetic variety. From the point of view of the economist such non-marketable items are 'externalities' and should not be entered even at estimated values.

Although the economist's case appears rational and consistent there are some difficulties with establishing an absolute discount rate. For example it appears that people are effectively using quite low discount rates (about 2 per cent) when they invest in education for their children — or even for themselves. This raises the question of what determines the time-perspective of individuals and of society as a whole. It seems likely that the perspective is strongly influenced by life-expectancy. To take an extreme, one could hardly imagine the mayfly (which lives only for one day) using a discount rate of 10 per cent p.a.! At the other end of the scale, those members of families which have enjoyed high standing, community responsibilities and a long tradition tend to identify themselves as custodians of that tradition and take a long time-perspective.

Nobody doubts the need for an adult (and therefore longer) time-perspective when caring for and educating the young. We try to persuade our children not to engage in pursuits that, though affording immediate gratification, will harm them in the long run. Similarly, we would like to think that our rulers and their advisers would take wise statesman-like decisions on our behalf, so that resources are conserved and we do not just live for today. Ultimately, this means that they must actually feel a responsibility for the longer term. However, the advisers have been trained above all to be rational and to discard mere emotional appeals. The New Vitalism indicates that on thoroughly rational grounds there is an excellent case for the existence of the soul and its persistence over much longer periods than threescore years and ten. We have a real vested interest in this planet for a lot longer than our current lifetimes. If we behaved as if this were true some of the grosser follies of the technologists would be avoided. I am not proposing that projects should be assessed using a zero discounting rate. I am suggesting that some things — such as the wholesale destruction of forests — that can be done (and are being done) should be regarded as beyond the pale. The possibility of their implementation should not even appear in the project assessment. Of all the messages that could be delivered to those in authority this is the one which, if taken to heart, would have the most far-reaching and beneficial consequences.

The Philosophical Message

Apart from messages at the personal level and those that bear on social issues, there are also implications for philosophy. Today's philosophers with their concentration on linguistics appear to be less concerned with the great issues than their forebears. However, it is striking that some of the most prominent of twentieth-century philosophers have great concern for topical issues. Bertrand Russell campaigned against the use of nuclear weapons, A. J. Ayer pleads for tolerance towards homosexuals, and Noam Chomsky inveighs against political corruption. No matter how stark the currently acceptable philosophical stance, there is room for consideration of the implications prompted by the New Vitalism.

One of the most intractable problems with which to wrestle is that of 'progress'. In terms of skills and technology it is not difficult to make a case for general progress by the human race over the past few millennia. With occasional periods of near-static societies and even the wholesale loss of skills and techniques as communities have been extinguished, there has been a steady advance culminating in a spurt during the past 300 years. Indeed the present-day ubiquitous products of technology point so clearly to progress in this field that it is easy to think of humankind itself as having also

progressed at the same rate. However, a pause to look more closely
at the political scene allows one to note that tyrannies flourish in
many parts of the world, as oppressive as any from the past. Perhaps our political institutions and particularly that of representa-
tive democracy are actually an improvement on the governmental
structures of primitive tribesmen but it is doubtful if this is immediately obvious to those at the lowest layer of the social hierarchy.
The idea of progress becomes particularly difficult to defend if it
is applied to the arts. There have been great flowerings of music
and the graphic arts within particular cells of time and space — as
if the muses had found little islands in time and space where they
could dwell happily. But when the flowering has passed there is
nothing left to celebrate but the records that remain. In the late
twentieth century our concert halls resound to the music of
Mozart and Beethoven — at the expense of contemporary com-
posers. Finally there is the area of personal relations. Are we more
polite to one another, more imaginative, more considerate, more
tolerant of each other's shortcomings? It is true that world opinion
condemns slavery (but it is still practised widely). The atrocities
committed in this century (such as those in Nazi Germany) have
been at least as vicious as any of the past. For every manifestation
of the advance of civilization it is not difficult to quote an instance
of modern barbarism. Overall it is difficult to make out a case for
sustained progress except in the fields of science and technology.

There have been many thinkers who find in this lack of dis-
cernible progress a source of depression — a terrible angst in the
face of such a comfortless spectacle. However, there is an alternative viewpoint. If you visited a school and you were told
gloomily by the staff that things were not improving — that indeed
it was necessary to teach the new arrivals all the old lessons that
had to be taught to the last generation of pupils — you would be
surprised, because that is the nature of a school. The New Vitalism
suggests that souls incarnate for the purpose of obtaining earthly
experience — as a sort of education. In addition to the arrival of
advanced pupils we have wave after wave of souls who are still at
an early phase of their education and going through the same
painful processes as their predecessors. Maybe on a grander time-
scale there is a sort of planetary progress and if one could watch
through hundreds of millennia there would appear a stately cosmic

advance. In the meantime there is the metaphor of the school within which appears quite a different interpretation for the rise and fall of civilizations. There is no need for that terrible pessimism which can grip one in the vain search for progress.

Chapter 1 contained a plea for a more open science which could move freely through all fields of investigation and not just those set by rather narrow traditions. Aside from the general desirability of a more open approach there is a strong argument for it which derives directly from the astrological findings of Gauquelin and the modern researchers. It has already been noted that the difficulties of 'discovering' astrology through a strictly empirical approach are so formidable that such a source for astrological lore is very unlikely. The astrological characteristics of the planets only come through strongly for rather special groups such as those investigated by Gauquelin. If collections of ordinary people were used for the base data then the apparent effects are so weak that any searcher without foreknowledge would come up with all sorts of spurious correlations and fail to assemble anything like the corpus of traditional astrology. Thus we have the extraordinary paradox of Gauquelin proving by means of a very exacting selection procedure followed by a fairly elaborate statistical analysis that the astrological nature of the planets accords closely with that believed by the ancients — and yet the kind of investigations they could have mounted would not have yielded correct findings. The only credible explanation is that the ancients had an alternative means of acquiring knowledge of the subtler influences.

There is a further consequence to be considered. If there had not existed any texts recording the ancient traditional beliefs of astrology it is extremely unlikely that Gauquelin or any of the other modern researchers would have attempted any statistical tests. By the standards of contemporary physical science with its limitations on physically possible causal links there can be no justification for spending any time and effort on chasing the superstitions of past ages. Thus we have a set of important discoveries which could have been initiated only by giving some credence to past visionaries or clairvoyants who declared there were connections between the planets and earthly life.

The next question to consider is whether this instance of a belief acquired by occult means and subsequently corroborated by detailed research is rare or indeed unique. There are some possible examples from the field of medicine. Quite a high proportion of the compounds used in modern medicine derive from plant sources and the plants have been long known to primitive communities for their medicinal properties. It can be argued that this elementary knowledge of plants could have been acquired entirely by empirical means (try everything and see what works) but this explanation has to be stretched to its limit when one realizes that the procedures for preparing the healing herbs were quite elaborate. The idea that it all came about as a series of happy accidents is difficult to accept.

The New Vitalism suggests that several of the beliefs which are contained in the major religions gain strong support from recent astrological research — particularly those related to the existence of a soul which pre-exists and also survives the body. The inference is that, far from being unique, the discovery of truths about the gross physical universe and also about the subtler features, through some visionary process, is not uncommon. One might well ask why science itself does not recognize this fact — and even make conscious use of it. The reason is that one of the roles which science plays is that of casting out superstition. Along with the pure gold of truth there is the dross of superstition. To the keen eye of our modern highly trained and sceptical scientist most if not all of the ancient beliefs are superstition. If asked to justify his position the sceptic can point to a long list of well-known superstitions starting usually with the widespread former belief in a flat earth.

What is interesting about this keen desire to root out all superstition, and to deny the possibility of knowledge being acquired by any other means than through empiricism, is that scientific discovery itself appears in many respects to share the same extra-sensory quality as the insights vouchsafed to the ancients. The accounts of discoveries written up for the learned journals are stories set out in acceptable logical format to provide a rationale for the event. They are often far from the real sequence of happenings. The typical inspired researcher is certain that he is right and sets out to prove it. If the first findings do not confirm it then he blames the apparatus or his technique or anything but the possibility that he is wrong. So convinced are some workers of the soundness of their insights that they will manipulate the results to make them more impressive. Clearly this does not appear to them as a dishonest act because they are only helping everyone else to realize something which ultimately will be accepted universally. It is now known that Gregor Mendel, the father of modern genetics, manipulated his findings to the extent that they were actually 'too good' statistically; i.e. his experimental figures were so close to the theoretical values that such a case could only occur very, very rarely and the charge of manipulation is effectively proved. Mendel's theory of inheritance was actually right and he is forgiven because it is a long time ago and he is not occupying a tenured post. The point is that such certainty about the truth of one's insights is not at all rare in the scientific community, and nor is the subsequent demonstration that the strongly held conviction was justified.

Insights can occur to scientists and they can occur to those who are outside of the scientific circle. We are prepared to award a special seal of approval to those which emerge from inside the circle because of the care taken to replicate and check the corroborative work, but it is a mistake to ignore all those insights which we have inherited from past ages. The message of the New Vitalism is that there is a gleaming trail of gold amid the dross and it is well worthwhile to continue prospecting.

In the earlier discussion of progress, reference was made to the way in which a flowering of artistic activity occurs within particular communities for quite short periods of a century or two. There would seem to be some reason for believing that a similar effect manifests in other areas of human interest. In seventeenth-century England at the time of the founding of the Royal Society a set of remarkable individuals made great strides in physical science, laying a secure base from which modern science could grow. It has been argued in preceding sections that insights which provide the seeds for major advances derive from a subtler realm — they are literally inspirations in the sense of the spirit communicating special messages. When the conditions are right it seems that there can be an outpouring of such inspiration to many individuals living contemporaneously in the same society. The inspiration which is currently manifesting in Europe and to some extent elsewhere in the world is the Green Movement. It appears most conspicuously as the emergence of Green parties in the politics of

European countries. Supporters of Green parties are strongly against nuclear weapons and nuclear power. They are suspicious of most high-technology enterprises. However, the Green Movement penetrates well beyond the overtly political arena and can be found in most aspects of living. Holistic medicine is making vigorous progress and alternative therapies such as homoeopathy and acupuncture flourish. Organic gardening, eschewing the use of artificial fertilizers and toxic sprays, has a growing number of converts. Diets which emphasize raw food, avoiding meat and even discarding all animal products, are becoming more widespread. A desire for crafted artefacts rather than those which are machine-produced appears to be increasing. Orthodox religion is in decline but there are signs of interest in versions of oriental religion with a strong emphasis on the practice of meditation. In the scientific field again there are some echoes of oriental religion with Capra's *The Tao of Modern Physics*[8] and a flavour of holism with Bohm's *Wholeness and the Implicate Order*.[9] In technology the work of Schumacher[10] has stimulated the initiation of appropriate technology and intermediate technology movements. A general environmental awareness is becoming widespread with emphasis on reducing pollution and avoiding damage to plants and animals. The rise of Greenpeace and the Animal Rights Movement is symptomatic of this trend.

The flowering of the Green trend covers so many fields that few people are left untouched by it, though there is a wide range of response. For every enthusiast who embraces all aspects of it there are scores who see virtue in only one or two of its manifestations. This is unsurprising because the Green Movement at heart is strongly spiritual in quality, emphasizing wholeness and the ultimate unity of the cosmos. The message of astrology, as outlined in this chapter, is in harmony with this concept of wholeness and unity. It is a message which is appropriate for the times in which we live. There is a general awakening to the deeper truths and this shows in a great variety of ways and through many channels — of which the New Vitalism is one. There is an essential unity of research activity. No real contradiction exists between, on the one hand, the scientific approach with its emphasis on physical evidence, and, on the other, those direct insights which occasionally illuminate the seeker after truth. Any apparent clashes are only transient and superficial — at a deeper level there is harmony.

Concluding Message

Astrology has many facets and the people who study it vary in their outlooks and their purposes. I doubt if many professional astrologers share the theories put forward in these pages. Only one member on the staff of the Faculty of Astrological Studies who was contemporary with me showed any hint of such leanings. This was Brigadier Ronald Firebrace, who remarked that he found it impossible to understand astrology without reincarnation. I do not think that he personally had memories which convinced him — he considered it a rational opinion in the light of the evidence. In the same way, the arguments put forward in these chapters are directed at those (like myself) who have no memories of past lives and no personal psychic powers. The New Vitalism is put forward for consideration as a theory with much evidence to support it. It may be wrong on some details, but overall I think the case is compelling and the messages derived from it are highly relevant to today.

REFERENCES

Chapter 1: Traditional Astrology

1. R. Sheldrake, *A New Science of Life* (Blond and Briggs 1981)
2. V. Clark, 'Experimental Astrology' in *Search* (1981)
3. M. Gauquelin, *The Truth about Astrology* (Hutchinson 1983)
4. J. Mayo, O. White and H. J. Eysenck, 'An Empirical Study of the Relation between Astrological Factors and Personality' in *Journal of Social Psychology* 105 (1978)
5. H. J. Eysenck at symposium on 'Astrology and Psychology' (University of London 1979)
6. K. Pawlik and L. Buse, 'Selbst-Attribuierung als differentielle-psychologische Moderatorvariable' in *Zeitschrift für Sozialpsychologie* 10 (1977)
7. *Biologist* (Spring 1975)
8. C. E. O. Carter, *Astrology of Accidents* (Theosophical Publishing House, London 1962)
9. G. Dean, *Recent Advances in Natal Astrology* (Analogic, Subiaco, W. Australia 1977)
10. A. Smithers, 'Testing Astrology's Key to Vocation', *Guardian*, 21 March 1984
11. D. A. Bradley, *Profession and Birthdate* (Llewellyn, Minnesota 1950)
12. J. Dieschbourg quoted in Dean, *Recent Advances in Natal Astrology* (ref. 9, above) p. 314 (ref. 8)
13. M. Gauquelin, *Written in the Stars* (Aquarian Press, Wellingborough, England 1988)
14. K. E. Krafft, *Traite D'Astro-Biologie* (Amedée Legrand, Paris 1939)

15. J. M. Addey, *Harmonics in Astrology* (Cambridge Circle, Wisconsin 1976)

Chapter 2: The Gauquelin Research

1. P. Choisnard, *La Loi D'Heredité Astrale* (Legrand, Paris 1939)
2. K. E. Kraaft, *Traite D'Astro-Biologie* (Amedée Legrand, Paris 1939)
3. M. Gauquelin, *The Cosmic Clocks* (Granada, London 1973)
4. P. Seymour, *Astrology: The Evidence of Science* (Lennard Publishing, Luton 1988)
5. S. Ertel, 'Grading the Eminence, or Raising the Hurdle for the Athletes' Mars Effect' (*Journal of Scientific Exploration* Pergamon 1988)
6. J. A. Hill and J. Thompson, 'The Mars–Redhead Link' (*Above and Below* No. 10, Stoyko and McRitchie, Ontario, Canada 1988)

Chapter 3: Wave Patterns

1. R. Courant, *Differential and Integral Calculus* (Blackie, London 1937)
2. J. M. Addey, *Harmonics in Astrology* (Cambridge Circle, Wisconsin 1976)
3. M. Gauquelin and F. Gauquelin, *Profession-Heredity, Series C, Volume 1* (Laboratoire d'étude des relations entre rythmes cosmiques et psychophysiologiques, Paris 1972)
4. C. G. Jung, *Synchronicity, an Acausal Connecting Principle* (Routledge, London 1955)
5. J. M. Addey, 'The True Principles of Astrology and their Bearing on Astrological Research' (*Correlation*, Vol. 1, No. 1, 1981)

Chapter 4: Theories

1. M. Gauquelin, *Written in the Stars* (Aquarian Press, Wellingborough, England 1988)
2. P. Seymour, *Astrology: The Evidence of Science* (Lennard Publishing, Luton 1988)
3. C. G. Jung, *Synchronicity, An Acausal Connecting Principle* (Routledge, London 1955)

4. D. Elwell, *Cosmic Loom: The New Science of Astrology* (Unwin Hyman, London 1987)
5. Rupert Sheldrake, *A New Science of Life* (Blond & Briggs 1981)
6. M. Gauquelin, *The Cosmic Clocks* (Granada, London 1973)
7. Y. Rocard, *Le Signal du Sourcier* (Dunod, Paris 1962)
8. F. A. Brown, jun., *Biological Clocks* (Heath, Boston 1962)
9. K. R. Popper, *The Logic of Scientific Discovery* (Hutchinson 1959)
10. M. E. Hone, *The Modern Textbook of Astrology* (Fowler, London 1950)
11. L. Kolisko, *Workings of the Stars on Earthly Substance* (Stuttgart 1928)
12. J. G. Toonder and J. A. West, *The Case for Astrology* (Penguin Books 1973)

Chapter 5: A New Vitalism

1. J. A. H. Waterhouse (*British Journal of Social Medicine*, Vol. 4, 1950)
2. J. G. Toonder and J. A. West, *The Case for Astrology* (Penguin Books 1973)
3. Michel Gauquelin, *The Truth about Astrology* (Hutchinson 1983)
4. G. Dean, *Recent Advances in Natal Astrology* (Analogic, Subiaco, W. Australia 1977)
5. N. Kollerstrom and M. O'Neill, *The Eureka Effect* (published by the authors 1988)
6. H. Driesch, *Mind and Body* (Methuen, London 1927)
7. U. Sinclair, *Mental Radio* (Laurie, London 1951)
8. R. Sheldrake, *A New Science of Life* (Blond & Briggs 1981)
9. R. Sheldrake, *The Presence of the Past* (Collins, London 1988)
10. H. P. Blavatsky, *The Secret Doctrine* (Theosophical Publishing House, 1897)

Chapter 6. The Message of Astrology

1. M. Grey, *Return from Death* (Arkana, London 1985)
2. K. Ring, *Life at Death: A Scientific Investigation of the Near-Death Experience* (Coward McCann & Geohegan 1980)

3. I. Stevenson, *Cases of the Reincarnation Type*, Vols. 1–4 (University Press of Virginia, Charlottesville 1975–83)
4. J. L. Whitton and J. Fisher, *Life between Life* (Collins, London 1986)
5. W. Shakespeare, *Macbeth*, V. v. 17
6. L. Timberlake, Sustained Hope for Development (*New Scientist*, 7 July 1988)
7. A. K. Dasgupta and D. W. Pearce, *Cost-Benefit Analysis* (Macmillan, London 1978)
8. F. Capra, *The Tao of Physics* (Fontana Collins 1976)
9. D. Bohm, *Wholeness and the Implicate Order* (Routledge, London 1980)
10. E. F. Schumacher, *Small is Beautiful: Economics as if People Mattered* (Blond & Briggs, 1973)

INDEX

Also in this series:

ASTROLOGY ALIVE!

Experiential Astrology, Astrodrama and the Healing Arts

BARBARA SCHERMER

Astrology is a powerful means of becoming self-aware. Barbara Schermer, whose psychological approach to astrology is strongly influenced by C G Jung, here puts forward an imaginative new way of furthering that understanding. She takes us on a journey through dance, music, art and drama so that the wisdom revealed by astrology is experienced as a living entity — astrology *alive!*

Using a wealth of exercises, rituals, meditations and games, Barbara Schermer breathes lives into the planets and signs and teaches astrological principles by experience. Ideal for individual or group work, this book captures the essence of the astrological influences and throws new light on their meaning in our lives.

'In *ASTROLOGY ALIVE! Barbara Schermer does exactly what her title suggests: she brings the astrological chart to life in a way that few other writers have done. It seems destined to become the classic textbook on experiential astrology. It certainly deserves to be.'* — Howard Sasportas

Barbara Schermer is a pioneer in the development of experiential astrology and an authority on astrological counselling and Kriya Yoga. She also co-ordinates astrology/psychotherapy groups and produces experiential theatre performances.

ASTROLOGICAL HEALING
The History and Practice of Astro-Medicine

REINHOLD EBERTIN

ASTROLOGICAL HEALING deals with the history and practice of astro-medicine, or 'cosmobiological' medicine. It chronicles astrology's application to healing from the earliest times and also covers Reinhold Ebertin's own invaluable work in this field.

The many links between astrology and alternative medical practices such as homoeopathy and biochemistry are clearly explained and Ebertin provides information about alternative healing techniques used in Germany today, how one can work with yin/yang foods for treatment, how cosmic factors play a part in illness and how to calculate a suitable day for surgery. This profound work will be essential reading for all serious students of astrology and the healing arts.

'As always with Ebertin, this invaluable work draws on the whole gamut of his lifetime experience as a practising astrologer/cosmobiologist. It is characteristically clear, direct and practical, showing how we can identify problem areas in the chart and how we can use astrology as an effective tool in the healing process' — Charles Harvey

Reinhold Ebertin (1901–1988) was one of the very great pioneer researchers, thinkers, innovators and organizers in astrology this century, emphasizing the great importance of social, environmental, educational, cultural and heredity factors in an individual's development. A prolific writer and author, he was also founder of the Ebertin Press and the annual Cosmobiological Research Conferences, and co-founder of the Cosmobiological Academy in Aalen. ASTROLOGICAL HEALING, his last major work, serves as an enduring tribute to his life.

Also available:

WRITTEN IN THE STARS

The Proven Link between Astrology and Destiny

MICHEL GAUQUELIN
Foreword by Professor Hans Eysenck
Postscript by Dr Geoffrey Dean

Michel Gauquelin's statistical studies of the birth data of thousands of famous people have been a key element in attempts to validate the claims of astrology.

He experimentally demonstrated the utter worthlessness of astrological predictions and personality descriptions. Seeking hard proof with which to back his experiments, he devised a most original and novel way of investigating astrological phenomena: he matched the birth data for thousands of famous people with their life histories — and succeeded in proving a relationship between personality and planetary positions at birth that defied normal explanation.

Thirty years after he first began to investigate the correlations between astrological data and life achievements, his experiments continue and positive results are still accumulating.

This book not only details the experiments but also provides material from the author's first two books, written in French and never before made available in English. The whole is a fascinating account of an impartially conducted study which appears to prove the validity of astrology and seriously threatens orthodox scientific thought — if true, it could dramatically change our conception of the universe.

RELATING

An Astrological Guide to Living with Others

LIZ GREENE

Since it was first published in 1977 this book has become a classic of modern astrological literature. Liz Greene's insights are as fresh and exciting as ever and the ideas she explores about the nature of relating have increased relevance today.

She shows how to use basic astrological concepts symbolically and practically, in a framework of Jungian psychology, to illuminate the ways in which people relate to each other on both conscious and unconscious levels.

RELATING remains a key text for any reader interested in the psychological dimensions of astrology; but it is also a book for anyone who wants to know more about themselves and the way they relate to others.

'*If you only read one astrology book this year, make it Liz Greene's RELATING . . . Even if you plan to read only one book of any kind this year, RELATING would still be an excellent choice.*' — Horoscope Magazine

'*A thoughtful and scholarly book which marries the profundities of Jungian psychology with the age-old science of astrology to provide fresh insights into ourselves and our relationships.*' — Psychology Today

'*A remarkably good book and highly recommended . . . this book deserves to be on every astrologer's shelf, if not on the shelf of anyone who cares about his or her relationships with others.*' — Prediction

THE ZODIAC FAMILY

How Astrology Can Help You Understand and Bring Up Your Child

JULIA PARKER

THE ZODIAC FAMILY is a guide to parenting that is meant to become dog-eared alongside your favourite childcare volume. It can be used to make informed decisions concerning your child — as a general guide to zodiacal tendencies or even in conjunction with a full birth chart.

This informative and often amusing guide offers helpful advice to any parents who want to bring out the best in their child as an individual, both at an early age and as he or she grows up. Children can also use the book to find clues to the tendencies of their parents, brothers and sisters.

In addition to lists of places, foods, plants, colours, and elements appropriate to the twelve signs of the zodiac, each Sun-sign chapter includes sections on:

Health and diet   Ideal careers
School years   Travel
Unemployment   Brothers and sisters

Julia Parker studied astrology following a career spent in art, dance, and teaching. She obtained the Diploma of the Faculty of Astrological Studies in 1967 and subsequently became the Faculty's President, a position she held for several years. She has been writing, with her husband Derek, since 1971 and runs a practice as a consultant astrologer, and her work has taken her all over the world lecturing and talking about her books.